EXPLORE
AND DISCOVER
MUSIC

EXPLORE AND DISCOVER MUSIC

Creative Approaches to
Music Education in
Elementary, Middle,
and Junior High Schools

MARY VAL MARSH

San Diego State College

The Macmillan Company
Collier-Macmillan Limited, London

Library of Congress catalog card number: 78-96743

THE MACMILLAN COMPANY
COLLIER-MACMILLAN CANADA, LTD., TORONTO, ONTARIO

Printed in the United States of America

To the loving memory of my mother

Foreword

Change is the order of the day. What kind of change is a matter for talk—talk in small meetings and large gatherings; talk set down on paper; and talk aired by the mass media. Except for isolated instances, however, the talk begins and ends in itself, offering little in the way of implementation to help one cope with each day's challenge.

Music teachers, like educators in all the disciplines, recognize the need for updating: curriculum content, teaching techniques, and classroom equipment, as well as attitudes toward children's interests and potential must be adjusted to the needs of a changing society. A view of how this may be done effectively is presented in this book.

Mary Val Marsh, calling upon long experience in teaching, has set down in these pages a kind of diary of her work with classes in the elementary school and junior high school. Were she to have written the book as a projection of what could be done in classrooms of the future, she could not have envisioned a more timely program for music education. The fact that this is a report of what has actually taken place in classrooms adds strength to its underlying principles.

Because Miss Marsh has worked with real children in real situations, she has a good understanding of what they can accomplish. In a totally practical manner, she provides specific information for teachers as to how children at all age levels can experiment to make discoveries that lead them to musical literacy.

For those who are interested in the subject, the book reads like an adventure story. Having begun it, I couldn't put it down. It is a fascinating account of true classroom happenings, much of it in conversational form, documented with details of procedures, equipment, titles of music, and scores of music children themselves have created and notated.

Here is a creative approach to music education that will serve not only teachers of today but those of tomorrow as well.

Beatrice Landeck

Preface

Explore and Discover Music grew from a desire to share with others the excitement that can result from helping students become actively involved in creating their own music. Enthusiasm from such participation may be equally strong in kindergarten, grade three, and grade eight. This same excitement may be felt by pre-service teachers in a music education class, or by in-service teachers participating in a workshop. The key to developing such interest in music is involvement of the individual in experiences that are meaningful and satisfying to him.

The major purpose of this book is to project some new dimensions in thinking about music education for children growing up in a period of unprecedented change and pressure. The book is not intended as a *method* or a *system* for teaching music, nor is it a bag of new tricks. It is not designed as a panacea for the problems that face teachers of music. In the opinion of the author, no such easy solution is to be found in any one approach to any curricular area.

Explore and Discover Music is designed with a two-fold use in mind. First, it is intended to serve as a professional stimulus and a practical reference for those engaged in teaching and supervising music, whether they are music specialists or general classroom teachers. For those with limited music background a glossary has been provided. Second, the book may be found valuable for music education classes. College students who become interested in exploring music materials and ideas and in developing their own music may be led to formulate important concepts about the discipline. As they find success in their accomplishments, some may conquer previously acquired psychological blocks to participation in music, and ultimately they may feel the need to symbolize their compositions in standard notation.

Suggestions for promoting musical creativity in students of all ages are given throughout the text, and summarized at the ends of chapters in sections entitled, "For Your Exploration." Related concepts also are listed following each chapter, to assure that activities will never become ends in themselves, but that students and teachers alike will use them as means of developing music literacy.

To acknowledge the help of all who have contributed to the contents of this book would be impossible. The ideas set forth have been acquired over a period of many years. The philosophy and practices embodied within the text are the result of professional contacts with a multitude of colleagues, both general educators and curriculum specialists in the fields of music, art, and dance. Some of the ideas that are discussed herein have undoubtedly been adapted from sources completely forgotten or unknown. To all who have in any way molded thought and practice as set forth in this book, the author humbly offers her gratitude.

In addition, special mention is due several associates who have contributed generously of their time to read, criticize, and discuss all or parts of the manuscript. To the following people the author is particularly indebted:

Dr. David Ward-Steinman, composer and Professor of Music, San Diego State College, for his perceptive criticism of the manuscript, and for information and inspiration in the area of contemporary music.

Beatrice Landeck, for her generous Foreword, and for encouragement during the earliest efforts with this writing.

Eloise Haldeman, music teacher, Beverly Hills Unified School District.

Madge Kamm, music and general classroom teacher, Claremont School District (California).

Eunice Seltenrich, music teacher, Hilltop Junior High School, Sweetwater Union High School District (California).

Lois Fair Wilson, specialist in early childhood education, Tucson.

Dr. Dwight E. Twist, Assistant Superintendent for Secondary Schools, San Diego Unified School District.

Grateful acknowledgment is made to the following organizations and individuals for photographs included in this book: Beverly Hills Unified School District; La Mesa-Spring Valley School District; San Diego Unified School District; San Diego State College Laboratory School; Danlee Mitchell, percussionist and music faculty member, San Diego State College; William M. Burgin, La Mesa, California; James Quider, Beverly Hills, California; William Threat, Highland, California; Peripole, Inc., Far Rockaway, N.Y.

Appreciation is expressed also to the MENC-Ford Foundation Contemporary Music Project, for the opportunity to carry on special projects dealing with contemporary music at the elementary and junior high levels, and to the Beverly Hills Unified School District for the opportunity to organize and teach the experimental program described in Part B of the book.

M. V. M.

Contents

EXPLORE
AND DISCOVER
MUSIC

Introduction

The rapidity of social change and the demands of young people to be *involved* in change have made it imperative that educational programs be reorganized and revitalized to meet the needs of today's youth. Giant strides have been made within the last decade to reconstruct goals and teaching procedures in certain curricular areas, chiefly mathematics, science, social studies, and language arts. Although some efforts have been made in the areas of music and art education, no major breakthrough has been seen. If music is to survive in the curriculums of American education, its goals must also be reconsidered, and its presentation revitalized so that it will become a truly significant part of the lives of boys and girls. This can happen only as teachers transmit to their students the excitement of *involvement in music,* of creating and recreating it. Music *does* have communicative powers, but these must be discovered by children themselves as they engage in meaningful exploration, and from their creative endeavors build concepts that are related to the total discipline. Exploration and discovery are as essential to music education as they are to other areas of study; an understanding of these processses can be a key to the improvement of music teaching.

Exploration and Discovery

These words characterize the latter half of the twentieth century, as man launches himself into a space age he is not sure he can control. Each day's newspaper tells of some new observation, experiment, formula, or mechanism which will make life more comfortable, or propel mankind ever faster into the realm of uncertainty. For many adults such rapid advances are unwelcome because contemplation of the unknown is often foreboding. Today's children, however, react quite differently.

The entire history of mankind has revolved around the processes of exploration and discovery. New lands have been settled and nations founded. Modern transportation and communication have shrunk the world unbelievably. Vaccines have emerged to control smallpox and poliomyelitis. Not many years ago the history textbooks referred to the fifteenth and sixteenth

1

centuries as the periods of exploration and discovery, and implied that there were few, if any, uncharted regions left to explore. Since the appearance of the atomic bomb and the accomplishment of space travel, however, the universe has seemed to open its arms to announce a new era for exploration, with wider horizons than could possibly have been conceived by Magellan, Cook, or Byrd. The resultant advances in science and technology have ushered man into a realm of living hitherto unimagined. Man is no longer confined to the Earth, or to the atmosphere that surrounds it.

Although these facts may be frightening to some adults, this new world is not a mystery to their children. The post World War II crop of boys and girls is as attuned to rockets and missiles, jet propulsion, and interplanetary travel as are their parents to locomotives, ocean liners, and automobiles. Since the spectacular landing on the Moon in 1969, children live on the brink of expectation that any day will bring news of earthmen landing on a new planet. This for them is not fantasy, but reality.

Nor are these space-age children mere observers upon the rapidly changing scene. Witness the numbers of science fairs which take place annually in public schools throughout the country, and stand amazed at the projects and experiments displayed by students. Their grasp of the world of science and the universe is staggering. They are not content merely to view the results of modern technology on television or the motion picture screen. Theirs is the desire to be on the inside, to play an active role in the process of change. Thus they prepare exhibits with titles such as "Ultrasonics," "Construction of a Laser," "Experimental Operation of Cloud Chambers," "Effects of Momentum on Seismic Intensity," and "Building a One Octave Electronic Organ," to the amazement of their parents and often of their teachers.

Although the world scene appears to be changing more rapidly today than ever in history, today's children are manifesting and reacting to the same basic drives that children have always felt as they have attempted to become a part of the society in which they have found themselves. Experimentation and exploration have always been major means by which youth have identified themselves with their culture, even though organized education often has been reluctant to capitalize upon active involvement as a way of accomplishing desired goals. Now it is apparent that educational approaches must become action-centered, and music education must keep pace.

Creativity in Music

In recent years educators have given increased attention to the development of the creative individual. Much writing and discussion has centered around the nature of creativity, the creative act, creative thinking, and the creative personality. The complexity of twentieth century living demands individuals who are able to cope with problems in imaginative ways, and who are not bound by static, preconceived patterns of thought and action. Thus it has become essential to find more creative ways of teaching that will in turn release the creative potential of those who are being taught. This would seem especially important in the teaching of music, a discipline that cannot exist apart from creativity.

The creativity that schools should be striving to develop in students may be defined as the ability to utilize materials and ideas in new ways. A creative product may be considered a thought, an act, or a construct that is original to its creator (though not necessarily to others). Although an extensive discussion of this vast topic is not feasible here, a few observations regarding creativity may provide a focus:

- There are many kinds of creativity.
- Creativity is a process as well as a product; the creative process may be of greater importance than the product created.
- Although the creative potential of various individuals differs as to degree and kind, creativity can be fostered in all human beings.
- Creative thought and action flourish in an emotional climate that is relaxed and accepting of individual response, as opposed to an atmosphere that is rigid and demanding of conformity.
- Creativity is promoted by a rich environment of ideas, experiences, materials, and equipment.
- Creative thought and action result from involvement of the learner in exploring ideas and processes.
- Success in creative endeavors motivates new creative pursuits.

From these general statements, a few implications may be drawn for fostering musical creativity in children:

- Creative musical expression may take many forms.
- The process of responding creatively in music may be more significant than a completed composition.
- All children can be helped to grow in their ability to be musically creative.
- The emotional climate of the classroom should cause children to feel free to respond musically in varied and original ways.
- The physical environment should contain music materials and equipment which students may explore and with which they may create.
- Students need to succeed in their creative musical endeavors; success often is realized in performance of that which is created.

When this meaning of *creativity* is considered, the role of *discovery* in creative learning can easily be seen and its importance recognized. Indeed the two processes are interrelated. Creativity is not possible without discovery, for when an individual thinks or acts creatively, he is discovering something previously unknown to him. As a child explores a given musical problem, he may think in ways that are new to him, and in so doing, make discoveries, or find solutions which he may then apply to further musical expression.

As music educators rethink the goals that seem of prime importance in a modern music curriculum, let them recognize that these objectives may best be achieved through creative approaches in which children are enabled to make their own discoveries. Too often music teaching has been organized with the idea that students will automatically be interested because they are *participating* through singing, playing instruments, or moving. Activity does not assure student interest, however, unless the pupil sees purpose in what he is doing. The confidence that results when a student is able to create a piece of music that he can play or sing, or develop a kind of movement that will express the meaning of a composition in a unique way, will bring about self-actualization and motivate participation in related activities. Thus it is possible to take a body of subject matter that seems essential to an understanding and true appreciation of music, and organize learning experiences by which students may "discover" the concepts considered vital. If the processes of learning are truly creative, the concepts which are formulated may not always be those anticipated by the teacher, but they will be related to the total discipline.

Conceptual Learning in Music

Although the term *concept* has assumed a myriad of meanings, it is commonly used in music education to refer to the formulation of specific and general ideas about the body of subject matter which comprises the discipline. This interpretation may imply that concepts exist in the cognitive domain only. If the teaching of music is approached from an intellectual viewpoint alone, however, all is lost, for without the development of concepts in the affective (attitude or value) domain, music becomes a lifeless entity, devoid of its primary aesthetic function. Music educators recently have begun to examine their field in an effort to pin down the major concepts that should form the basic subject matter of music education. Emphasis has been upon cognitive objectives, perhaps because they have seemed a bit more tangible. Hopefully the time is not far distant when music concepts will be clarified for the affective domain, and the psychomotor domain as well. The latter, involving motor skills, would seem tremendously significant for the area of music education.

It is not a goal to present herein a hierarchy of concepts that should be the aim of music education. The major purpose of the volume is to suggest a variety of approaches by which pupils at various stages of musical and chronological development might be guided to make discoveries about music, and gradually conceptualize their learning experiences. The classroom examples cited are intended to show how various classes or individuals became involved in exploring the media and materials of music, and to suggest ways by which other classes might be guided into similar experiences. Although the discoveries will differ with each group which participates, they will of necessity be related to the total body of knowledge, appreciations, and skills which comprise musical learning. Thus students will make their own discoveries, formulate their own specific concepts, and gradually generalize their concepts or broad understandings.

The concepts given at the end of each chapter are in no way intended to represent a comprehensive coverage. They are selected concepts which students might be helped to formulate, depending upon the focus given to the particular exploratory experience. In order to provide the reader with a frame of reference, however, the following rationale regarding the nature of music is presented.

The Nature of Music

The prime ingredient of music is *sound*. Sound is the *sine qua non* of music. It is sound which sets music apart from all other art expression. Musical sound often is referred to as *tone*.

Sound consists of four components, without which it does not exist. These components are *duration, pitch, timbre,* and *volume*. Every tone that is sounded exists for a particular duration of time, be it long or short. Every tone has some pitch, whether high or low, definite (tuned) or indefinite. Every tone has a particular timbre, or tone quality, characteristic of the medium, or instrument, which produces it. This medium may be a human voice, a traditional instrument, or a sound source as yet unaccepted or undiscovered. Every tone has a level of volume, or degree of loudness. When tones are sounded sequentially, *tempo* (rate of speed) is present.

Duration and pitch are organized and combined in a variety of ways to produce *rhythm, melody,* and *harmony,* and these in turn are combined and organized into musical *structures* or *forms.* Performance media are utilized in many combinations to create a variety of *timbres* or *tone colors.* Volume is controlled to produce constant or changing dynamic levels. Many kinds of *textures* result from combining rhythms, melodies, and harmonies in various ways. Musical meaning is increased as controls of *dynamics* (loudness and softness), *tempo* (fastness and slowness), and *articulation* are exercised.

The chart on page 6 may help clarify thinking regarding the nature of music and the process by which random sound is organized into music. Unorganized sound is noise. And, although it might *not* be agreed that *all organized sound is music,* it is unquestionably true that *all music is organized sound.*

```
                        ┌──────────┐
                        │  SOUND   │
                        ├──────────┤
                        │  (TONE)  │
                        └──────────┘

   TIMBRE      DURATION        PITCH      VOLUME


                    TEMPO


TONE COLOR    RHYTHM    MELODY    HARMONY    DYNAMICS
(TIMBRE)


                    TEXTURE


                        ┌──────────┐
                        │   FORM   │
                        ├──────────┤
                        │ (MUSIC)  │
                        └──────────┘
```

SUMMARY

Music education must become more attuned to the needs and interests of today's children and youth. Music teaching must utilize more fully the desires of students to be actively involved. This may be accomplished by providing situations in which boys and girls create, as well as recreate, music which has meaning to them. Students need opportunities to explore the media and materials of music, to make discoveries regarding the nature of music, to create many kinds of music, to conceptualize their learnings about music, and to apply their concepts to new musical ventures.

Part A

Exploring Sound—
Discovering Music

The world of sound holds untold fascination for children of all ages.

Chapter 1

Unorganized and Organized Sound

We live in a noisy world!

A shattering blast is felt. An explosion? No. Merely a shock wave, caused by a plane exceeding the speed of sound. Sonic booms are within the daily experience of a multitude of human beings, who, although they may wince at the strongest tremors, have learned to accept them as an inevitable phenomenon of the age in which they live.

So it is with the screech of brakes warning of a possible crash, the competitive rumblings of household appliances, and the conglomerate background of sounds created by radio and television. Few human activities are carried on in the absence of sound. In fact the experiencing of complete silence can be extremely frightening. Thus we acknowledge that sound is inseparable from the environment in which human beings exist.

The frequency, diversity, and intensity of environmental sound seems ever-increasing, especially in highly urbanized areas. The human being, in an effort to preserve his emotional stability, is forced to *tune out* those sounds that have no particular significance to him. For the youngster living in crowded quarters, it becomes a matter of school survival to learn to study amid television, family conversation, traffic, and the baby's crying. The housewife, concentrating on the comparative value of two cuts of meat at the supermarket, shuts out of her conscious hearing the background music provided (although admittedly there are times when its presence helps sooth jangled nerves). Thus the individual gradually is conditioned by his environment to eliminate from his conscious thought all sounds that do not have direct bearing on his interests and activities.

Not so with the newborn infant, even an infant arriving in the twentieth century. To him each new sound is a mystery and a marvel. He soon learns that he can be the creator of sound itself. A baby's cries, gurgles, and jabberings reflect his daily discoveries of rhythm and pitch in a multitude of combinations and variations which he finds himself able to produce. He quickly observes that by altering rhythm and pitch in certain ways he can communicate his feelings to others. His rattles and hard-surface toys become his means for increasing the volume of his communication.

The world of sound holds untold fascination for children of all ages. The "Brrrrr, brrrrr, brrrrr" that accompanies play with a toy airplane, the continuous "Ding-a-ding-a-ding" of a tricycle bell, and the monotonous scuffing of the toe of a shoe against a wall are manifestations of an inner urge to create repeated sound patterns. With his voice, with his toys, with objects from his environment, today's youngster explores sound as children have always done. But the space-age child interprets his findings in terms of jets, nuclear blasts, and rockets to the moon. He is attuned to the new era in science, and music education for this child needs to be on the same frequency.

Tuning In to Sound

Steve suddenly stopped reading, and the entire group turned to see why.

"Hey, what's that noise? he questioned, rising to peer out of the window. Several others joined him.

The first-grade teacher also rose to observe a pile driver at work on an addition to the school plant. The children had watched attentively during preceding weeks as the ground has been cleared of an existing structure, excavated, and otherwise prepared for the foundation of the new building. This great machine, however, was new to the scene, and thus it generated tremendous excitement.

It was obvious that interest in the activity outside had broken the spell cast by the printed page, so the teacher said wisely, "I think we should take a walk in order to watch and listen to the big machine. It's called a pile driver. Watch and listen carefully, and when we come back we'll see how much you've found out about the way it works and the sounds it makes."

The group of eager six-year-olds moved to the grassy plot adjacent to the work area. For nearly fifteen minutes they sat and studied the operation, often making observations to each other. Upon their return to the classroom the teacher led a short discussion regarding the function and operation of the equipment, and then asked for volunteers to show in movement how the pile driver worked. Several individuals presented their ideas, and then someone suggested that at least four people were needed to portray the operation accurately.

When the group seemed satisfied with the reproduction of the shape and movement of the machine, the teacher asked, "Is something missing?"

"There isn't any noise," replied one child. By this time the real machine had stopped, and there was comparative quiet.

Hey, don't forget the cymbals!

"What kind of a sound do we need?" questioned the teacher. "Loud or soft?" "High or low?" "Continuous, or starting and stopping?"

The group agreed that the sound was loud, sharp, rather low in pitch, and steady in rhythm. After some experimentation it was decided that an adequate reproduction of the sound could be produced on two deep-toned tub drums, two deep-toned wood blocks, and cymbals. The sounds were added to the rhythmic movement, and although considerable practice still was needed to improve coordination, the group seemed genuinely delighted with the results. These six-year-olds had been helped to become not only visually and aurally observant of their physical environment, but also creative in reproducing the shape, movement, and sound of this particular phenomenon.

The foremost job of each teacher of music, whether a music "specialist" or a general classroom teacher, is to open children's ears. Without the ability to distinguish one sound from another a child is unable to sing in tune, clap or play a rhythm pattern accurately, or recognize an oft-heard orchestral theme. This principle applies to any individual at any age. Conversely the more highly developed the powers of aural differentiation become, the greater will be the ability of the individual to sing difficult vocal lines, reproduce complex patterns in rhythm and analyze masterpieces of the orchestral repertory. The ability to perform or consume music will be in direct proportion to the ability to discriminate aurally.

Aural perception comes about gradually as individuals recognize likenesses and differences among sounds. Initial discoveries involve pitch, duration, tone color or timbre, and volume. Students need a wide range of opportunities to explore and create sound in order to grow in musical acuity.

Young children delight in their discoveries of the differences in the sounds that they create.

Using Environmental Sound in the Classroom

Reproducing environmental sounds for songs, stories, poems, dramatizations, and sound pictures can increase children's discriminatory powers tremendously. Voices, hands and feet, percussion instruments, and sound-producing objects which children bring to class need to be explored and re-explored many times before satisfying reproductions are discovered. Disturbing as it may be to the teacher, the final choices of the group may seem not at all satisfactory to her. This may be an indication that the sounds being reproduced are not sufficiently familiar to the children's ears, or that the group needs to become better acquainted with the timbres of the instruments or objects being used. On the other hand, children may discover many possibilities which have never occurred to the teacher, and which reflect *their* impressions of the world of which *they* are a part, rather than those of the teacher's world. For, environmental sound has a direct relation to the culture which produces it, and thus might even be considered an important key to the understanding of history.

Exploring Sound Through Literature

The "sound words" in the following poem were obvious to a third grade group after one reading:

There was an old witch, Believe it if you can,
    She tapped on the windows and she ran, ran, ran.
She ran helter skelter with her toes in the air,
    Corn stalks flying from the old witch's hair!

"Swish," goes the broomstick; "Meow," goes the cat.
    "Plop," goes the hoptoad sitting on her hat.
"Whee," chuckled I, "What fun! What fun!"
    Halloween night when the witches run.[1]

"Could you suggest some sounds which might be substituted for certain words in this poem?" asked the teacher.

"We could rub our hands together when we say 'swish'," said one of the group.

"Sand blocks sound like 'swish' too."

"Or the Indian rattle!"

[1] From *This Is Music*, Book II, by William R. Sur, Mary R. Tolbert, William R. Fisher, and Adeline McCall. © Copyright, 1967 and 1961, by Allyn and Bacon, Inc. Used by permission.

"Good suggestions," encouraged the teacher. "What about other words?"

"Me-ow," came a kitty-like squeal from the back of the room.

A boy unable to wait any longer clapped his cupped hands together as he grunted, "Plop!"

"We could play that big drum real loud for 'Plop,' " suggested still another.

All ideas were tried, with combinations of sounds finally substituted for the words mentioned, plus several others. Over a period of time, enrichment was added by giving the poem a choric speech treatment. The group was divided into lower- and higher-pitched voices, and several solo parts were used. Changes in dynamics and tempo were discussed, and the final organization of voices was as follows:

There was an *old* witch,　　Believe it if you can,
　(All low voices, very softly)(One voice, skeptically)

　　She tapped on the windows and she ran, ran, ran.
　　　(A few voices, lightly)

She ran helter skelter with her toes in the air,
　(High voices, excitedly)

　　Corn stalks flying from the old witch's hair!
　　　(All voices, loudly)

　"Swish," goes the broomstick; "Meow," goes the cat.
　　　(All voices)　　　*(One)*　　*(All)*

　　"Plop," goes the hoptoad sitting on her hat.
　　　　(All)

　"Whee," chuckled I, "What fun! What fun!"
　(One)　　*(All)*　　　*(One)*

　　Halloween night when the witches run.
　　　(All)

The alert teacher will look for many poems and stories with possibilities for the creative use of sound. The following poems might be used with children in ways similar to those just suggested.

Tumbling Jack

Tumbling Jack goes clickety-clack,
　Down the ladder and then comes back.
Clickety-clackety, rattle and hop,
　Over and down again, flippety-flop!

Unknown

New Year's Eve

FIVE . . . FOUR . . . THREE . . . TWO . . . ONE . . .
>   MIDNIGHT!

It's gone forever
That happy old year,
With Christmas, Thanksgiving, and Fourth of July.

Sound horns, ring bells,
Cheer and strike gongs.
When I look back, will I laugh or cry?

Clash metal on metal,
Make a festival noise.
Will new days creep slowly or lift off and fly?

Let's welcome this moment,
This Happy New Year,
With Christmas, Thanksgiving, and Fourth of July.

>   *Matthew Alden*

A Quiet Time

Up in my room
I can sense more than hear
The tip-tip-tipping
Of shy falling rain.

Molly the Mama-cat
Two feet of stretched fur
Saws syncopated logs
With comic refrain.

The clock holds it's rhythm
But doesn't intrude.
It tells me that this time
Is mine—all mine.

A few broken chords
On my brand new guitar
While the world outside
Is benign.

>   *Susan Lucas*

I Rode on a Jet

I rode on a jet,
The biggest one yet.
It roared like a lion
When it left the ground,
But when it was high
There wasn't much sound.

    I rode on a jet,
    The biggest one yet.[2]

I rode my black horse,
We circled the course.
From stable to stream
We challenged the wind.
Crossed over the bridge
And raced 'round the bend.'

    I rode my black horse,
    We galloped the course.

I rode on a ferry,
It was slow and not scary.
We loaded the cars
Like toys in a box,
And chugged 'cross the bay'
As waves lapped the rocks.

    My ride on the ferry
    Was slow and not scary.

    Susan Ward-Steinman

Song of Summer[3]

A thrush in a bush:
    "Lirra-Lirra-ling!"

[2] First verse from *Exploring Music,* Kindergarten Book, by Eunice Boardman and Beth Landis. © Copyright 1969 by Holt, Rinehart, and Winston, Inc. Used by permission.

[3] From *Winds A' Blowing* by May Justus. Poem copyright 1952 by the Sunday School Board of the Southern Baptist Convention. Used by permission of Abingdon Press.

A cricket in a thicket:
"Zing-zing-zing!"

A frog in a bog:
"Boom-boom-boom!"

A bee in a blossom:
"Zoom-zoom-zoom!"

Listen-Listen!
There's music all about.

Does anybody want to sing
or whistle-or shout?

May Justus

Exploring Sound Through Songs

The idea of using sound effects with songs is not new, but still is valuable as a means of stimulating the aural imagination as well as promoting coordination. Songs dealing with transportation, machinery, construction, animals, wind, ocean, and clocks often lend themselves to such treatment. Children should be encouraged to discover appropriate sounds. The three following songs are examples of those which are suitable for sound effect enrichment:

GIDDAP, OLD DOBBIN [4]

WORDS AND MUSIC BY
BEATRICE AND MAX KRONE

I like to drive the horse and bug - gy, When I go trav - 'ling to the town; I like to hear old Dob - bin's clip, clop, I like to feel the wheels go 'round.

Sound: "Clip-clop" of Dobbin's hoofs (Wood block, cocoanut shells, or inverted paper cups).

[4] From *Discovering Music Together*, Book 4, by Charles Leonard, Beatrice Perham Krone, Irving Wolfe, and Margaret Fullerton. © Copyright 1966, Follett Publishing Company. Used by permission.

OLD HOUSE [5]

AMERICAN FOLK-GAME SONG
COLLECTED BY JOHN W. WORK

1. Old house. Tear it down! Who's going to help me? Tear it down!
2. New house. Build it up! Who's going to help me? Build it up!

Bring me a ham-mer. Tear it down! Bring me a saw.___
Bring me a ham-mer. Build it up! Bring me a saw. ___

Tear it down! Next thing you bring me, Tear it down!
Build it up! Next thing you bring me, Build it up!

Is a wreck-ing ma - chine. Tear it down!
Is a car-pen-ter man. Build it up!

Sounds: Wrecking (Experiment by scraping guiro or notched wood block;
striking drums, wood block, or tambourine; shaking maracas
or rattles.)

Building (Try sand blocks, wood blocks, and deadened metal objects
such as a cowbell.)

Before moving from the topic of instrumental enrichment of songs, three
points need to be made. First, a song should be learned thoroughly before sound
effects are added, lest attention be diverted and the song be learned incorrectly.
Second, the accompaniment should always be kept subordinate to the song. This
will require sparse instrumentation with young children. Third, the creation of
sound effects for songs should be distinguished from *percussion accompaniments*
intended to be representative of various countries or culture groups. (Examples
of the latter are given in Chapter 2, pages 50-55.) Sound effects can be created
with any instrument or object which simulates the desired sound satisfactorily.
On the other hand instruments used to provide an accompaniment indigenous to
a culture should be as authentic as possible, in order that students do not form
misconceptions. Papier mache around a light bulb may produce a fine rattle for
sound effects when the light bulb is broken inside the dried paper, but it is a
rather inappropriate substitute for maracas to accompany a Latin American
song.

[5]From *Music in Our Town,* by James L. Mursell et al. © 1956, 1962, Silver
Burdett Company. Used by permission.

THE SONG OF THE RAIN

WORDS AND MUSIC
BY MARY VAL MARSH

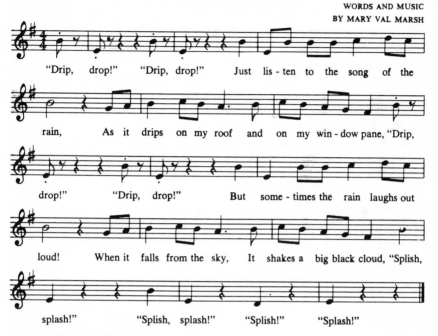

"Drip, drop!" "Drip, drop!" Just lis-ten to the song of the rain, As it drips on my roof and on my win-dow pane, "Drip, drop!" "Drip, drop!" But some-times the rain laughs out loud! When it falls from the sky, It shakes a big black cloud, "Splish, splash!" "Splish, splash!" "Splish!" "Splish!"

Sounds: "Drip, drop" (Sticks, high wood block, fingers on desks).
      "Splish, splash" (Rattles, sand blocks, palms of hands).
      Thunder (Drums).

Creating Pictures and Stories in Sound

Sound effects used to enrich songs often can be organized into an improvisation in sound, or a "sound picture." A fourth-grade group, enjoying a Halloween song, decided to accompany it with appropriate spooky noises—rattling bones, howling wind, moaning ghosts, and creaking doors. They discussed the importance of keeping these effects in the background, subordinate to the song, in order to create a true "accompaniment." The effect was so exciting that they decided to expand their efforts to include a dramatization. They considered possible settings, such as a graveyard, a deserted castle, and the top of a dark mountain. The last was chosen by a majority.

It was midnight, just before the witching hour. A tick—tocking clock (which many of today's children have never heard!), whistling wind, and the chime in the tower striking twelve were chosen as a fitting introduction to set the mood for the song. As ideas developed, the sounds became so exciting that the song no longer was needed. The following story sequence evolved:

At the striking of twelve, ghosts appeared and began to roam about. A screech owl cried, a black cat leaped across the fence, and a witch flew by on her traditional broomstick. A rattling sound then introduced the skeletons who gradually shook themselves loose from their graves to begin a gay dance. They were joined by several cats—black, of course—and were having a merry time, when suddenly the great clock struck "One" and all movement ceased. Now no sounds were heard except the moaning wind and the creaking door.

Such a story, developed by children, can be told in sound alone or with the addition of dramatization, preferably without words. These experiences serve not only to stimulate children's "sound imaginations" but also to promote their growing awareness of certain aspects of compositional form, especially the need for climax.

Another subject that usually is of interest to students of all ages is sounds of early morning. This offers unlimited possibilities for imaginative uses of familiar sounds, and can be short enough for five-year-olds, or sufficiently challenging for a junior high group. These two examples will illustrate:

Following a discussion of sound and music[6] the teacher said to a second grade class, "Let's pretend it's early morning. Close your eyes and see what sounds your mind hears which could be reproduced on one or more of our percussion instruments. When you've decided you may play it for us to guess."

The choices were:

Alarm clock	Triangle
Bird	Light bells on stick
Little brother playing	Tambourine
Scraping shoes	Sand blocks
Mother sweeping porch	Sand blocks
Footsteps of sister walking down the hall	Drum
Church bells	Triangle
Two dogs barking	Drum and voices

When played in sequence, with no comment, the effect was "really good," as stated by one of the class members. These sounds proved doubly useful, for they were then added to a song by being substituted, two at a time, for the third line. The song was "Wake Up."[7]

A seventh-grade group put together a lengthy sequence with some sounds difficult to describe on paper. It happened that there was an extremely talented extemporaneous narrator in this class. Therefore the sequence of

[6] From *Experiments In Musical Creativity*, published by the Contemporary Music Project of the Music Educators National Conference, © Copyright 1966. Used by permission.

[7] In *Music in Our Town*, by James L. Mursell et al., Silver Burdett Company, 1962.

sounds listed below (as recorded by the students for a reminder) is punctuated by a few of the accompanying comments:

Sound	*Instrument(s)*
Crickets ("before you hear them, but they're there")	Hand castanets (Handcastas)
Telephone ("five times, soft to loud")	Bells on stick
Cat purring ("one-half hour later; I went back to sleep")	Balanese straw shakers
Wind	Sand blocks
Palm branch hitting, then scraping window	Drum—strike, then scrape with fingernails
Target shooting practice	Drums
Father coming downstairs ("must have lots of money today")	Bells and tambourine
Coffee pot ("Mother wants coffee; Father can't drink it—he has ulcers!")	Oriental temple blocks
Tractor and hammer ("Housing project next door")	Guiro and wood block
Sonic boom ("always during breakfast")	Several drums
Dishwasher	Maracas and wood block
Brushing teeth	Sand blocks, one edge rubbed against another block
Hurried footsteps	Wood block
Door slam	Sand blocks hit together
Starting car ("it's a *very* old car!")	Tambourine—shake and hit
Car blinker	Temple blocks
...and Awa___y we go!"	

Often a sound picture will develop without a definite story sequence, with just a mood to be expressed. Stimulating subjects which can be explored include a storm, sounds of the city, a deserted beach, the airport, a festival, and space sounds.

The latter idea was utilized in a summer workshop of teachers as they were attempting to show through rhythmic movement the revolution of the planets within the solar system. One member suggested that some space music would add immeasurably and thus a small group who had been experimenting with percussion instruments began to create appropriate sounds. It is again difficult to describe in words the effectiveness of the results. The instrumentation was thin, producing an ethereal feeling. The improvisation began with a slow, repeated tone played on one of the highest of the melody bells. Someone joined with a faster, uneven (short-long) pattern played on two temple blocks (high to low). An occasional quick scrape on the guiro, scattered glissandi up and down the melody bells, a fast five or six note pattern on a very high wood block, three strikes on a large cymbal with a mallet and a few circular swishes of the sand blocks were combined to create a stunning setting for the movement of the planets.

As stated, the outer-space effect seemed to be achieved through the thinness of instrumentation and irregularity of the sounds played. Nothing was written down in traditional notation. Both instrumentalists and dancers projected themselves into the mood they wished to create and the empathy between the two groups was remarkable. The space music idea is fascinating to students, especially to those in intermediate and junior high grades. A recording of *The Planets* by Gustav Holst may be used effectively in conjunction with such experiences.

A tape recorder can prove invaluable in helping students of all ages hear and evaluate the total effect of a sound accompaniment, sequence, or story that they have created. A fourth-grade class developed a sequence based upon playground sounds. Their ideas were listed on the board, and the sequence was practiced and changed several times. When the performance had been polished to the students' satisfaction, it was recorded on tape. The class was pleased with the result. Several weeks hence someone mentioned the tape and the class asked to hear it again.

"Do you remember all the sounds you were imitating?" asked the teacher.

Quickly came the response, "That doesn't matter; let's just listen to it for the sound!"

Hearing Environmental Sounds in Composed Music

Sounds of nature and the immediate environment undoubtedly have always held a fascination for man. Thus it would be expected that the composer, in his quest for new sounds, should incorporate environmental sound in his music. Although this practice reached its zenith in the descriptive music of the Romantic Period (roughly, the nineteenth century), examples of the programmatic use of sound can be found nearly as far back as recorded music.

A brief search will reveal that compositions inspired by the natural environment are so numerous as to defy listing. Among more familiar examples are the following:

- *La Mer (The Sea)* by Debussy.
- *The Moldau (The River)* by Smetana.
- *Clouds* by Griffes.
- *The River* by Thomson.
- *Three Outdoor Scenes* by Ives.
- *Death Valley Suite* by Grofe.
- Symphony No. 6 ("Pastoral") by Beethoven.

At least four composers produced larger works which they entitled *The Seasons* (or *The Four Seasons*), as follows:

Vivaldi—four miniature violin concertos.
Haydn—an oratorio.
Glazunov—a ballet.
Tchaikovsky—twelve piano pieces.

In many instances composers have attempted to simulate *specific* environmental sounds through appropriate instrumentation. A few random examples are as follows:

The Birds (dove, hen, nightingale, cuckoo) by Respighi.
"Hens and Cocks" (from *Carnival of the Animals*) by Saint Saëns.
"From the Diary of a Fly" (from *Mikrokosmos,* Bk. VI, No. 124) by Bartok.
The Little Fly by Couperin.
"Little Train of the Caipira" (from *Bachianas Brasilieras No. 2*) by Villa Lobos.
Steel Foundry by Mossolov.

Still other composers have gone so far as to call for a *literal* reproduction of an environmental sound. The song of the nightingale has been simulated both instrumentally and vocally by countless composers including Couperin, Beethoven, Stravinsky, and Clokey. Respighi, however, wishing to capture the true beauty of this sound in his "Pines of the Janiculum" from the *Pines of Rome* suite utilized a *recording* of a live nightingale singing. A second grader, when asked how he thought it possible to include the song of a live bird in a composition so that the song would be heard at the right time, said, "I guess he was a well-trained bird."

George Gershwin, captured by the quaint charm of French taxi horns, scored a section of *An American in Paris* for four tuned taxi horns, which can be purchased with the score. Other composers who have called for literal sounds are Mozart—sleigh bells in "Sleigh Ride" (from his *German Dances*); Tchaikovsky—cannon in *Overture Solennelle* ("1812"); and Handel—fireworks in the original performance of his *Royal Fireworks Suite.*

The Search for New Sounds in Music

Above are but a few examples of compositions in which environmental sound has played an important role. Utilization of such sounds is not limited to descriptive music, nor to the music of any period. Indeed, the modern orchestra is the result of the composer's eternal search for completely new sounds, or for new ways of using sounds already at his disposal. (Chapter 4 is devoted to the contemporary search for new sound.) Children can be helped to understand this attempt to utilize all sound possibilities by creating their own "new sounds" and by putting them together in organized ways.

Creating with "Built-in" Sounds

A group of nine-year-olds were discussing the instruments of the woodwind family, that they had just seen and heard at a school assembly. One curious boy asked, "What was the first instrument ever played?"

"Does anyone know the answer?" inquired the teacher.

"It probably was a hollow log, maybe with a skin stretched over the end like a drum."

"I read a book someplace about a Greek boy who found a reed in a swamp and blew into it and that was the first instrument."

"Like the man today blowing into the soda straw and cutting it off to change the pitch. That was neat!"

"Think about it, and do some research tonight. Tomorrow I might be able to bring a recording of the *very first* instrument," suggested the teacher.

The following day, after giving the students an opportunity to exchange ideas, the teacher said, "Here is a recording using an instrument I believe was the very first. See whether you can discover what it is."

Hands began to be raised after a few seconds of "Variations on a Handmade Theme" by Warren Benson. As the title had not been disclosed prior to the listening, the children guessed "drums," "wood blocks," and "some kind of wooden clappers" before someone gasped with the correct answer. (Some groups will immediately identify the *instrument* as hands clapping.)

"Undoubtedly the first instrument was the human body," said the teacher. "Let's see how many different kinds of sounds can be made starting with hands and feet."

The first sounds suggested were clap, snap fingers, rub palms, slap legs, tap feet, and stomp feet. This list was extended to include vocal sounds of a tongue click, sssss, and ssshhhhh. The teacher held a chart of some rhythm patterns which the group had created several weeks before, and suggested that these patterns might be orchestrated with the sounds just listed. Although this seemed a minor challenge at first, the students soon found that considerable concentration and coordination were required to execute the performance. The score was "orchestrated" as follows:

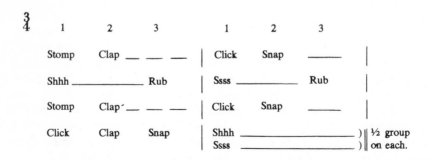

Such experiences with rhythm scores orchestrated for "built-in" sounds can be begun in the lower primary grades through clapping with appropriate songs, clapping rhythm patterns to imitate the teacher and other students, creating appropriate vocal sounds effects, and gradually notating some of the less complicated rhythms produced. For example:

(A)   Shhh   𝄾 | Shhh   𝄾   ‖ (With a song)

(B)

(Rub palms together to simulate old steam engine sound)

(C)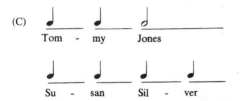

(D)   _____ X   X | _____ X   X ‖
      Clap   Snap Snap | Clap   Snap Snap

(E)   Shhh: _____ _____ | _____ _____ ‖
      Clap: ___ ___ ___ _____ | ___ ___ ___ _____ ‖

Instruments are extensions of sounds which human beings can make with their own bodies. As children exhaust the latter possibilities they may find new sound-producing media by exploring objects in their environment.

Composing with Original Instruments

The air was filled with a multiplicity of noises created by hitting, scraping, blowing, rubbing, pulling, and shaking. The fifth and sixth graders were exploring an odd assortment of objects called by them "original instruments." There were bowls of many sizes, shapes, and materials. Other kitchen items included graters, egg beaters, plastic jugs and bottles filled with rice, sugar, and dried peas, coffee cans with plastic lids, and a pair of wooden spoons that gave a sharp resonant sound when hit together. A girl had talked her father into bending a long rusty curtain rod into a triangular shape. When the over-sized triangle was struck with a metal spike, the rich resounding tone could be heard for "12 whole seconds" by accurate ten-year-old timing.

A boy had created a one-string violin that had eight fret marks for plucking an approximation of a diatonic scale. There were several sets of tuned bottles and glasses of varying pitch and timbre (tone quality) and assorted bells. The pride of the group was a conch shell on which its owner was able to blow an impressive tone.

Everyone had contributed at least one instrument, and although there was great variety, nearly all objects met the following criteria, which had been established the previous week:

All original instruments must:

1. Have an interesting and potentially "musical" tone.
2. Be durable.
3. Produce a sound that can be heard across the classroom (though not necessarily a loud tone).
4. Be as attractive as possible.

Students had been cautioned against the use of rubber bands, cardboard boxes and other weak, non-resonant materials.

"As you demonstrate your instruments would you indicate to which of these groups they belong," requested the teacher, pointing to columns labeled *Strike, Shake, Scrape, Blow, Pluck.*

After all instruments had been shown it was found that the largest number belonged in the first column. It was noted, also, that instruments which were struck produced two kinds of tones—*stopped,* as was the case with most wooden and plastic objects, and *resonating,* usually produced by metal and glass objects.

Instruments were compared with regard to pitch as well, and lists were made of those considered to be *high, medium,* and *low.* All instruments except the few wind and string ones were then related to familiar percussion instruments found in an orchestra.

"How could we use these fine instruments most effectively?" asked the teacher.

"We could make a composition for them, like some of the ones we've listened to," replied one student.

"Yeah! It could have different parts for the shakers and strikers and scrapers," offered another.

"Well, I think it would be more interesting to have the instruments mixed up," said a third.

Your own composition sounds much better
when it is played on "original" instruments.

After a bit more discussion, the teacher said, "Much music has been written for separate groups of instruments, such as strings or woodwinds. In orchestral music, however, the sections usually do not play alone for very long. An entire composition divided in this way might not 'hang together' or have a feeling of being unified."

"I think it would be better to use different kinds of sounds in each section," agreed another student.

As this class was accustomed to working in small groups for many purposes, it was decided to proceed in this way to create sections for the composition. Thus four groups were organized arbitrarily. A student was selected from each to be chairman and notate what his group created.

Students were reminded of the *standards* they had previously established for working in small groups. The teacher also mentioned that it would be necessary for each group to decide upon a general plan for using its instruments. Would all play at the same time? Would they write a rhythmic theme for each classification of instruments within the group? Or, would one or two begin to play with others entering at specified times? The term *texture* was discussed in relation to the kind of sound that various combinations might produce. The teacher suggested that each group begin by choosing a meter.

Students eagerly moved to their designated areas, with many playing their instruments en route. Soon, however, the groups began to work seriously on the assignment. One group decided to have each person create a rhythm pattern that could be repeated as an ostinato. The chairman numbered the members in the order in which they were to enter and drop out. As there were nine in the group, it was decided that each person should play his pattern ten times, then stop. This would provide two measures for all to play together and, tactfully, would give everyone the same number of measures to play. Several of the patterns were as follows:

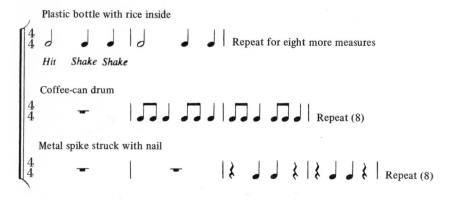

Another group, looking for a ready-made solution to the problem, decided to play the rhythm of a familiar song—"Pop Goes the Weasel." Instruments with contrasting timbres were given different phrases, with several "surprises" playing the "pops."

The group working nearest the above-mentioned one had less imaginative leadership and when they overheard the idea of using the rhythm of a familiar tune, decided to follow suit. They chose "Billy Boy," and despite their lack of originality in the initial planning, the results were quite effective. The "strikers" played

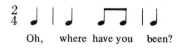

They were joined by the shakers on

The next phrase,

I have been to seek a wife

was given to the bent curtain rod triangle, with

for the part - ner of my life

going to the four tuned and suspended bottles, which played

The last phrase was played by all in a grand finale:

She's a young thing and can - not leave her moth - er.____

The fourth group contained one very talented child who suggested to his peers that he could improvise on his handmade xylophone. (He had found time to cut only four bars to "exactly the pitches I wanted.") The other students, he felt, could play ostinatos during his improvisation. He met his match, however, in the girl who had brought the conch shell and who was not about to be relegated to the minor role of accompanying him. She told the group that an ostinato on her instrument would "drown out everyone else," and she felt the shell could be used much more effectively to play an impressive introduction and a coda. Thus the final composition consisted of two notes from the shell, three ostinatos (two children playing each), over which there was an improvisation, followed by two more horn-like tones from the conch shell. The score is shown on page 30.

The groups completed their planning in fifteen minutes. They made little attempt to notate their compositions at this time, except for some long and short lines (blank notation) to help them remember patterns. Groups one and four, which created patterns of their own rather than using familiar melodic rhythms, could have utilized more time to practice. They were able, however, to demonstrate their ideas to the rest of the class.

Although each group was most interested in its own effort, all students were attentive to and appreciative of the performance of their peers. They were anxious to have more time to work out their ideas in practice, and thus the

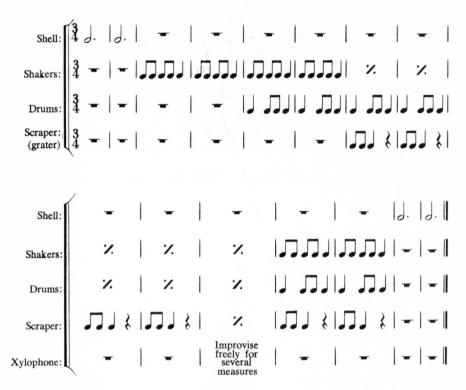

teacher provided time on succeeding days for polishing and for accurate notation of scores.

When results were shared later, there was evidence not only of pride in small group work, but also of the accomplishments of the class as a whole. Wishing to build on this spirit, the teacher asked, "Can you think of any musical form we could use to put all four of these percussion compositions into a single larger work?"

The response, "A rondo," came quickly, for the class had been listening to short compositions in rondo form and discussing the meaning of the term. It seemed a logical way to utilize four different sections. The next job was to decide in what order the sections would appear.

The composition of the first group described above was chosen as the "A" section of the rondo. This effort consisted of a series of nine ostinatos. The composition based on the rhythm of "Pop Goes the Weasel" became "B," the improvisation composition was entitled "C," and the "Billy Boy" variation was called "D." The final form was A B A C A D A—an "extended" rondo. Thus the knowledge of a musical form which had been gained through previous listening and moving to music was reinforced through this simple percussion composition created by students for their original instruments.

Although older students can choose and construct sound-producing objects with more discrimination than younger children, the discovery of new sounds can be just as exciting for primary children as for the ten- to twelve-year-olds described above. A second grade group created the following composition[8] with their original instruments:

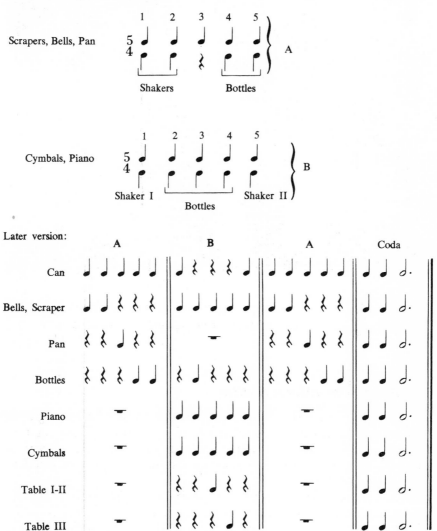

[8] From *Experiments in Musical Creativity,* published by the Contemporary Music Project of the Music Educators National Conference. Copyright 1966. Used by permission.

Percussion instruments must be explored many times before their potential is realized fully.

Exploring Instrumental Timbres

Before children are able to use percussion instruments with any degree of discrimination, whether for sound effects or other purposes, they must be familiar with the timbres of the various instruments. Much of this understanding will come about through exploratory activities such as those described throughout this chapter.

It is important, however, to plan specific time at all grade levels for children to explore instruments, compare them, and learn to play them correctly. Some of the concepts which children should develop through such experiences are the following:

    1. Most percussion instruments are played by striking, shaking, or scraping (rubbing) them. (See the Appendix for names of specific instruments.)

2. Some percussion instruments produce tones which resonate for a considerable period of time. Others produce a tone which seems to stop almost immediately.

3. Percussion instruments of metal tend to resonate longer than those made of wood.

4. Nontunable instruments can produce tones of different pitches, depending upon the materials used and the size of the instrument.

5. A larger instrument will tend to produce a lower tone than the same kind of instrument smaller in size. For example, a large drum usually will produce a deeper tone than a small drum constructed of like materials.

If consistent effort has been made from kindergarten on to sharpen children's awareness of sound in the natural and man-made environment, in song and speech, in literature, in instruments, and in the music they create—indeed, in all of life's activities—there are no limits to which students can grow in their musical understanding. For, *music* defined most broadly is *organized sound.*

CONCEPTS RELATED TO CHAPTER 1

1. Sound exists in both the natural and the man-made environment.
2. Individual sounds possess audible characteristics.
    a. Each sound has a characteristic timbre, or quality.
    b. Each sound has duration and exists only in time.
    c. Each sound has a pitch level.
       (1) Sounds that are nontuned have relative pitch.
       (2) Sounds that are tuned have definite pitch; these sounds are referred to as *tones.*
    d. Each sound has a level of volume.
3. The composer is continually searching for new sounds with which to create music.
4. Instruments are extensions of sounds which can be made with the human body.
5. Most percussion instruments are played by striking, shaking, shaking, or scraping. (Additional concepts related to percussion instruments are found above in the discussion, "Exploring Instrumental Timbres.")
6. Music, most broadly defined, is organized sound.

With Sound—Encourage students to:

· Listen for environmental sounds; describe their qualities verbally (for example, *loud, sharp, whirring, jerky, rumbling*).
· Gather sound-producing objects that make interesting and unique sounds; emphasize their tone qualities, to develop aural perception.
· Find appropriate uses for these sounds in songs, stories, dramatizations.
· Create *sound stories,* that is, communicate an environmental setting or sequence of events through sound (for example, "Another Halloween," "A Journey Through Space," "A New Day," "The House That Was Haunted," "A Storm in the Forest," "The Harbor Trip").
· Identify real or simulated environmental sounds in composed music.

With Percussion—Encourage students to:

· Discover "built-in" sounds which they can produce (for example, clap, snap fingers, click tongues, rub hands together, tap feet); use these in rhythm compositions.
·Imitate various rhythm patterns which the teacher claps or plays on a percussion instrument; initiate their own patterns for others to answer.
· Create instruments that produce interesting, unique, resonant musical sounds; use these as the instrumentation for original rhythm compositions.
· Explore and describe verbally the timbres of percussion instruments available in the classroom.
· Classify these instruments in various ways:
    Duration: stopped vs. resonating tone (for example, wood block vs. triangle).
    Pitch: higher vs. lower (small drum with high pitch vs. large drum with low pitch).
    Sound production:
        Striking (drum, wood block, triangle, cymbal, gong, tambourine, claves, castanets).
        Scraping or rubbing (sand blocks, guiro, notched wood block).
        Shaking (tambourine, rattles, maracas, sleigh bells).
· Create original compositions for percussion instruments.
· Identify timbres of percussion instruments heard in recorded compositions.

With Recordings* mentioned in this chapter:

Bartok, Bela, "From the Diary of a Fly" from *Mikrokosmos,* Bk. VI (No. 142) (Vox SVBX 5425, 3-record album).

*Because of the rapidity of change in availability of commercial recordings, it is suggested that a catalog or a record dealer be consulted before ordering recordings listed here.

Beethoven, Ludwig van, *Symphony No. 6* ("Pastoral") (Columbia MS 6549; Victor LSC 2614).

Benson, Warren, "Variations on a Handmade Theme" (on *Warren Benson Presents,* Golden Crest GC 4016).

Couperin, Francois, "The Little Fly" (on *The Birds and the Bees,* Musical Heritage Society MHS 766).

Debussy, Claude, *La Mer (The Sea)* (Angel 35977; London 6437; Columbia MS6077).

Gershwin, George, *An American in Paris* (Capitol P 8343; Victor LSC 2367; Columbia MS 6091).

Glazunov, Alexander, *The Seasons* (London 6509).

Griffes, Charles, *White Peacock* (Mercury 90422; also on *Adventures in Music,* Gd. 6, Vol. 1, RCA Victor).

Grofe, Ferde, *Mississippi Suite* (Capitol P 8347; also on *American Scenes,* Bowmar Orchestral Library BOL 61).

Handel, George Frederick, *Royal Fireworks Music* (Columbia MS 6095; Victor LSC 2612).

Haydn, Franz Joseph, *The Seasons* (DGG 139254-6; 3 records).

Holst, Gustav, *The Planets* (Westminster 14067; London 6244).

Ives, Charles, *Three Outdoor Scenes* (Composers Recordings Inc., CRI 163).

Mossolov, Alexander, "Steel Foundry" (or "Iron Foundry.") (on *Sounds of New Music,* Folkways FX 6160).

Mozart, Wolfgang Amadeus, "Sleigh Ride" from *German Dances* (Mercury 90438; Angel S 35948).

Respighi, Ottorino, *The Birds (Gli uccelli)* (Mercury 90153).

Respighi, Ottorino, "Pines of the Janiculum" from *The Pines of Rome* (Columbia MS 6587; Mercury 18035; London 21024).

Saint Saëns, Camille, "Hens and Cocks" from *Carnival of the Animals* (on *Animals and Circus,* Bowmar Orchestral Library BOL 51).

Smetana, Bedrich, *The Moldau* (Victor LSC 2471; Mercury 90214).

Tchaikovsky, Peter Ilyitch, *Overture Solennelle* ("1812") (Columbia MS 6827 or MS 6073).

Tchaikovsky, Peter Ilyitch, *The Seasons* (Columbia CML 4487; transcribed for orchestra).

Thomson, Virgil, *The River* (Vanguard 2095).

Villa Lobos, Heitor, "Little Train of the Caipira" from *Bachianas Brasilieras No. 2* (Victor LM 1994; also on *Adventures in Music,* Gd. 3, Vol. 1, RCA Victor).

Vivaldi, Antonio, *The Four Seasons* (Columbia MS 6195; Angel S 35877).

Chapter 2

Exploring and Discovering Rhythm

African drum talk

Continuous circles in the pattern of a beach umbrella

The rough, smooth, rough, smooth, rough, smooth
feel of a newly turned ceramic pot

Repeated clicking of a stone caught
in an automobile tire

Do-si-do and a grand-right-and-left

A heartbeat

So vast is this world of rhythm and so basic to human life that no justification need be given for finding effective ways of helping students discover some of its many facets. Rhythm can be seen, felt, and heard. Without it there would be no art, no dance, no music. Without its beat there would be no life.

Every individual has his own rhythm. Some people are much more able than others to translate this inner rhythm into overt actions such as clapping, foot-tapping, and dancing. The differences are quickly apparent to anyone who works with young children. Let us not assume, however, that because Bobby, age five years, has difficulty in learning to skip, to paint rhythm into a design, or to play a drum with regular beats that he "has no rhythm in his soul." He may need only a little more time to mature. Repeated opportunities to move, paint, and play the drum, though unsteadily at first, will help develop needed coordination.

Children must be helped to move freely before significant interpretation of music is possible.

Bobby, as all Bobbies and Betties like him, needs *time* to grow rhythmically. He needs time, and equipment, and space, to experiment without pressure to conform to a design, pattern, or tempo set by the teacher or even by his peers. Bobby should have continuing opportunity, whether he is five, eight, or fourteen years old, to meet rhythm in a multitude of situations that have meaning for him. Seeing, hearing, touching, painting, and moving to rhythm are all important if he is to develop a comfortable natural rhythmic response. How essential for true artistic and musical growth that Bobby discover rhythm with his *heart* as well as his *head!*

Exploring Rhythm Through Movement

Rhythm begins inside the human being. The heartbeat which is basic to life differs among individuals. Nonetheless it is present in every living person. The baby uses his entire body to express his feelings long before he can make them known verbally. Most civilizations have recognized the dance as a basic medium for giving expression to human emotion, both in individual and group form. How logical that educators should capitalize on and develop this built-in medium of movement for teaching rhythm.

Moving to music can be a powerful force in unlocking expression only if the individual is *free* to be sincere in the interpretation. Bobby must be helped to be honest in his dancing as he portrays what the music says to him, rather than being encouraged to "be an elephant" when he may never have seen a live elephant. A dance teacher once said, "Moving like a bunny does not necessarily create 'bunny-ness.' "

Music speaks with a strong pulse, with the lightness of feathers, in jerky angles, through smooth crystal-clear strains. As Bobby becomes increasingly able to *describe* the *qualities* of music he hears instead of trying to *be* something superimposed by a title on a record label, he will gain the confidence necessary for sincere and honest expression.

The teacher asked, "How does it feel to be a balloon?"

"Light."

"Bouncy."

"Puffed up."

"It feels tied to a string."

So answered four small individuals from a group of children ages four through eight.

"What else can you think of that feels light and bouncy and puffed up?" questioned the teacher.

"Puffed rice," said one, thus disclosing his favorite breakfast fare.

"Clouds," replied a more wistful child.

"Pufferbillies," laughed a curly-headed blond boy who was built like one.

"When you hear this music you may dance the lightest, bounciest, puffiest thing you can imagine. This is your chance to feel like puffed rice, or clouds, or duck feathers, or whatever you can think of that fits the feeling of the music. Listen for a minute before you start to move."

With the opening strains of "Laideronette, Impératrice des Pagodes" from *Mother Goose Suite* by Ravel, most of the group caught the mood and floated off about the room. The movements were varied. Some felt lightness through small, delicate foot patterns, and others through whirling motions with arms extended outward and upward. The pufferbilly boy, seeing that his friends were concentrating on the music, soon took hold of a new idea and began to bounce vigorously. One small member of the class doubled herself into a roundish shape and gently tossed and swirled in lovely patterns about the room.

After the music had stopped and the children were gathered for discussion the teacher asked, "Would anyone like to tell us how he felt as he danced?"

At which point the "small one" replied, "I felt like a great big dandelion puff dancing with the wind."

Through many experiences of this type in which emphasis is upon the inherent quality or character of the composition rather than upon a story or programmatic idea, children's attention is turned to the music and away from themselves. Gradually self-consciousness disappears, as the criterion for success is not gracefulness or realism but the extent to which the movement is a sincere and convincing expression of the spirit of the selection. No two expressions will be alike, for this is a personal response. Creative dancing which thus begins *inside* the individual will in no way resemble the awkward, superficial motions that usually result from teacher-imposed ideas.

As children become increasingly free in their movement, more attention can be given to the structural aspects of the music. For example, students moving to the "Bear Dance" by Bartok soon may discover that some members of their group are showing the underlying pulse or beat, while others are dancing the rhythmic pattern of the melody. Seeing the following notation may help develop a concept regarding the relationship of rhythmic pattern to pulse:

This learning can be transferred to other listening experiences not involving movement and also to familiar songs. Note the similarity of the pulse and pattern notation above to the following song excerpt:

FOOBA WOOBA JOHN

Pulse:

Saw a flea kick a tree, Foo-ba woo-ba, foo-ba woo-ba,

Children also will begin to recognize repetition and contrast in the music they are dancing. Movement now can take on greater organization, as different groups may be needed to indicate various themes or sections of the composition. Thus movement becomes a means for developing concepts regarding musical form. (See Part B for an account of the use of movement to develop understanding of musical form.)

Exploring Rhythm Through Art

"What is a line?"

"Who can draw one with his hand?"

"With chalk?"

"With moving feet?"

These questions and others from the teacher of a group of nine- to eleven-year-olds stimulated a fascinating series of experiences dealing with line, and later with color in music, art, and dance.

The question, "What can a line do?", led to a multitude of responses:

"It can curve."

"Goes up and down."

"It could make a circle."

"How's about a zig-zag!"

Many ideas were shown on the chalkboard, by arm motions, and by large locomotor movements across and around the room.

Jane illustrated, "This one makes sharp points":

"What name might we give this other than a line?", asked the teacher.

"It could be mountains," said Betty.

"Looks like sharks in the ocean," replied Wilson.

The teacher pursued the idea. "Let's draw it in the air and see what we feel."

After considerable exploration, Phyllis exclaimed, "Y' know, it's just like a rhythm. It makes a pattern."

This experience was taking place in the school cafeteria. A nine-foot length of butcher paper had been cut and rolled for each child and broken pieces of chalk in assorted colors were available. The paper rolls were arranged in four wide circles with a large box of chalk in the center of each circle.

"We're going to hear some music now, and then on those rolls of paper you may draw any kinds of lines suggested to you by the music. Use about this much of the paper for each painting," said the teacher, indicating a two- to three-foot length, "as there will be several records. Here is the first. As you listen to the selection think about the kinds of lines you will use."

The class listened thoughtfully, with attention that surprised even the teacher, to "Nuages" by Debussy. After one hearing, with no further discussion, the children were excused to find a place to draw and were encouraged to work only as long as necessary to achieve the desired effect.

There was an amazing lack of curiosity about the work of others. The students were intent upon the task at hand. Nearly everyone drew large, flowing, undulating lines which created some exciting patterns. Some did the entire painting in one color and achieved interest by varying the width and intensity of the lines. Others mixed colors quite successfully.

The second selection, "Polka" from the *Age of Gold* ballet suite by Shostakovitch, brought sharply contrasting results. Now the lines used were short, jagged, and angular, and colors chosen were somewhat brighter than for the first composition. Many children captured the detached, staccato quality of the music through repeated spotted and dotted patterns.

"Danse Russe" from *Petrouchka* by Stravinsky stimulated some remarkable representations. It was apparent during the listening preceding the painting that the children were excited about the music. The art that followed portrayed slashing, dry, ragged designs done in wonderfully strong colors. The enthusiasm for the music was so high that several students suggested moving to it.

Most of the group responded to the idea, including several who had been reticent heretofore to participate in movement. As they returned from some rather strenuous dancing one fifth grader panted, "Gosh, that's the first time I've really felt *in* the music."

The Related-Arts Experience

A word regarding the relationship of the arts in the classroom program seems in order at this point. The so-called "related experience in art and music" for which many teachers provide time often lacks quality as an educational experience in either field. Seldom do the art results evidence feeling for the basic quality of the music, or are they the best possible art expressions. Instead the paintings usually attempt to portray the story around which the programmatic musical selection is built. Undoubtedly the pictures could have been produced as well or better from a purely verbal rendition of the story, although perhaps the music added mood which may have been reflected in the art results.

The above statement is not intended as a condemnation of the idea, but rather as a plea to the reader to analyze the *basic purpose* for the related experience. Is it primarily an art experience, with music serving to set a mood or relax the students or reinforce a story idea? If so, concentration should be upon art expression and technique. Or is the intent to use art as one medium for expressing mood, components, or structural design within the music? If this is the case, all attention should be given to the process of listening first, without the distraction of mixing the right color or drawing a horse's tail effectively.

Both seem legitimate experiences if the goals are kept clearly in mind and the results are both musically and artistically genuine, rather than superficial. Any such combined activity should be preceded by considerable experience with both music and art per se.

Hearing, Dancing, and Painting Rhythm

There was an air of excited expectancy as the sixth grade class entered the large multipurpose room. At one end was a phonograph with some carefully chosen recordings beside it. At the opposite end of the room were long tables arranged to allow space for painting. Three sheets of 18" x 24" manilla paper were placed for every child. For each pair of students there was a tray containing three art media—colored chalk, tempera (powder paint) in three colors (with additional colors available from a nearby table), and small sponges for application, and finger paint mix to which desired color could be added. The group had worked previously with all three media mentioned. A large rag and a can of water were included with each tray. As students were shown the art materials it was explained that any one medium could be used after hearing and then moving to a particular selection of music.

The children sat on the floor around the phonograph.

"We've learned a lot about rhythm lately," began the teacher. "Where have we found rhythm?"

"In our classroom—the windows, tile in the floor . . ."

"That wood paneling on the wall over there."

"Folk rock has it!"

"The waves of the ocean as they break have rhythm, too."

"What about our drums? We make rhythm with them," responded the expert bongo player of the class, almost defensively.

The teacher continued, "And what do we find is the result of repeated or organized rhythm, whether in a painting, or a musical composition, or a dance?"

After some discussion it was decided that the organization of rhythm resulted in a shape or design or form.

The teacher said, "Today we'll concentrate on hearing and feeling rhythm in the music, and then translating this rhythm into designs in space through movement, and into patterns on paper through painting. Although other aspects of the compositions will be reflected in your dancing and painting, try to concentrate today upon *rhythmic design.*"

This class had previously had many opportunities to move to music. They had begun with bouncy music, such as the folk dance version of "Pop Goes the Weasel" and selections from a recording entitled *My Scotland,* concentrating on the feeling of bounce down deep inside themselves. They had discovered that when the feeling came from inside the individual, the entire body interpreted the rhythm and mood, instead of arms and legs alone.

The teacher had worked for sincerity of expression in slow and sustained music, such as "Arioso" by Bach and *Clouds* by Griffes; in ponderous selections, as "Jimbo's Lullaby" by Debussy, and "In the Hall of the Mountain King" by Grieg; and in light, airy pieces such as "Badinere" by Bach and "Dance with Pennons" by Rogers. Getting descriptive words from the children as they listened had helped develop their powers of concentration, their abilities to verbalize their feelings, and, in turn, their abilities to express their ideas in movement with the entire being.

For this listening-dancing-painting experiment, the teacher decided to use other favorites, chosen for rhythmic variety. Selected were "Children's Dance" by Hanson, *Fantasia on Greensleeves* by Vaughan Williams, and *España* by Chabrier. The children were told the first number would be played twice for listening and moving, and twice for painting, as it was of short duration. This was the "Children's Dance," included because of its bouncy beat and its syncopation. The movement and painting that followed reflected in some measure both these aspects of rhythm. It was interesting to note that many of the students who showed syncopation in their dancing also caught it in their paintings. This was not true in every case. Most of those who responded in movement to only the pulse of the music, however, painted the same steady kind of rhythm. Nearly all of the art work used bright, gay, warm colors, and no one chose to work with finger paint at this time. Most of the designs were done in chalk.

The Vaughan Williams number elicited movement and painting that were in sharp contrast to expressions resulting from "Children's Dance." This was to be expected. Only the first section of the composition, utilizing the "Greensleeves" theme, was played. Both movement and painting reflected the gentle flow of rhythm, with occasional swirls and turns indicating melodic contour and dynamic change. Large colored scarves were provided for those who wished them for dancing. Much finger paint was chosen for this selection and greens, blues, and purples were predominant. During the painting one student was observed as he captured the rhythm of the harp accompaniment which coincides with the pulse. His patterns followed a $\{ \}$ design. Later he wove through these the flowing line of the melody.

España was a favorite for movement. Nearly everyone wished a scarf, and the few tambourines offered were eagerly sought. Sweeping turns and swirls marked the free spirit of this music, as students used space from the floor to the tops of their up-stretched finger tips. Although they stopped the dancing reluctantly, the same freedom soon was reflected in their painting, done, for the most part, with tempera and chalk. There were, however, several striking finger paintings, two of them in red. Most of the responses emphasized the strong accent on the first count of each measure. One girl portrayed the pulse of the music with a ♩ ♩ ♩ design. To this she added shapes, representing the pattern of the second and third counts (♩ ♪ ♩).
                                                                                                    1 2 3

The flowing rhythm of the "B" section was then woven around and through these basic designs.

Student reaction to the experiment was not difficult to ascertain. The question asked most frequently during the remainder of the day was, "Can we do it again tomorrow?"

The experience just described necessitated a great amount of preparation, as well as adequate space for freedom in both dancing and painting. A two-hour block of time was also required. Many of the same values can be obtained through lessons not as involved—for example, through the use of a single art medium. Students should be well-acquainted with any art materials chosen, and better results usually will be achieved with music that has been used for movement on previous occasions. Music must be selected with care, for it is difficult to find compositions suitable for both dancing and painting.

Whatever the choices of physical setting, music, and art media, carefully planned and purposeful experiences in related listening, movement, and art can bring about significant learning in all three areas.

Discovering Rhythm in Speech

For fifteen minutes the teacher-observers squirmed while ten six- and seven-year-olds explored. Each child was holding a drum and making good use of it.

"You may have some time just to enjoy your drum," commented the demonstration teacher. "See how many ways you can find to play it."

For fifteen uninterrupted minutes they played, some continuously, while a few individuals left the group momentarily and then returned. They beat the drums with heavy strokes, tapped them lightly, slapped them briskly.

Occasionally two children would accidentally establish counter-rhythms and would find their accident quite enjoyable.

Peter exclaimed, "Hey! Do you know you can even get a sound from the wood part?"

Although interest was sufficiently high that the activity could have continued indefinitely with worthwhile results, the inevitable dismissal hour was not far away and the teacher thus stopped the playing.

"What are drums used for?" she asked.

The anticipated responses were given, among them, "To march," "In a parade," and "My brother plays one in the orchestra."

"The Indians used them," offered Karen.

"What for?"

"Hunting."

"War drums!"

"To send messages. They talked with them."

The teacher said, "I'm going to make my drum talk to you. To what part of you might it speak?"

"Our feet," said several.

And so the children were led by the drum to walk and run and skip in response to its voice. One week earlier the same group, when given an opportunity to move to some recorded music with the help of brightly colored scarves, had proceeded to choose their scarves with care, place them neatly on the floor and sit on them. Either these children had never before been freed to move to music, or the gay scarves held a greater fascination at the moment than the particular selection of music. Now, however, the voice of the drum could not be ignored.

"My drum will say something else now. Can you tell what it says?" asked the teacher as she played:

"That says, 'I want to,' " volunteered a small redhead.

"You want to *what*?" replied the teacher.

Feeling the restlessness which comes to six-year-olds at 11:50 A.M., Bruce said with definiteness, "I want to *go home*."

$$\frac{4}{4} \; \music$$

"I want to *go home*, I want to *go home*," echoed the drum. "And what will you do when you get home?" asked the keeper of the drum.

"Eat Lunch!"

"Watch T.V."

"Can you play these words on your drums?"

And suddenly from sixes and sevens three rhythm patterns emerged simultaneously:

I want to GO HOME, I want to GO HOME,

Eat lunch, Eat lunch

Watch T. V., Watch T. V.

The first fifteen minutes had been well spent in *exploration* leading to *discovery*.

How many different sounds can you make on your drum?

The close relationship that exists between rhythm in music and rhythm in speech is obvious. In reference to songs, it should be considered an *interrelationship,* which too often has been ignored by composers and arrangers of vocal music. Natural accents of words and melody must coincide if the result is to be an adequate musical expression. A quick look at some song collections and choral arrangements may reveal startling examples of songs consisting of "unwed" words and melodies.

Children can become sensitive to the natural rhythm of words through the use of drums and other percussion instruments as just described. Another favorite drum game is that of playing the rhythm of students' names and then discovering those which are alike. For example, "Timothy Jones" could be played,

$$\frac{6}{8} \quad \sqrt{} \quad \sqrt{} \quad \sqrt{} \quad \int.$$

Tim - o - thy Jones
Su - san De - Witt

as could "Susan DeWitt." "Roberta Smith," on the other hand, could not. Although the number of syllables in the name is the same, the natural accent is on the second syllable rather than the first. In $\frac{6}{8}$ meter "Roberta Smith" might be played,

Ro - ber - ta   Smith, Ro - ber - ta   Smith

Another name with like accent is "Patricia Snow." By combining the two patterns shown, a simple polyrhythm is developed:

Many names seem to fall most naturally into a $\frac{2}{4}$ or $\frac{4}{4}$ meter, as shown:

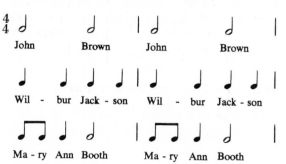

John   Brown   John   Brown

Wil - bur Jack - son   Wil - bur Jack - son

Ma - ry Ann Booth   Ma - ry Ann Booth

This type of activity can be used with any proper names, such as rivers or states, or with any category of words. The purpose is simply to sharpen awareness of accent, and of the fact that there is rhythmic pattern in speech. Such awareness can be extended through work with various kinds of poetry based on both regular and irregular rhythm. Space does not permit further discussion of this topic here. Related ideas, however, are considered in Chapter 1 (Exploring Sound Through Literature) and Chapter 3 (Sing a Story, and Setting Haiku to Music).

What Is Rhythm in Music?

Rhythm is a basic ingredient of music. It is often referred to as one of the elements of music. It appears, however, that the element (sine qua non) might better be thought of as *duration,* for every tone exists only as it is heard in time.

The term *rhythm* has a broader connotation and implies the *organization of duration* into

- pattern—combinations of long and short durations.
- pulse (or beat)—regularly recurring stress.
- meter—groupings of pulses (and patterns) into 2's, 3's, and combinations thereof, by means of accent.

The activities described throughout the first part of this chapter emphasize the importance of helping children become aware of rhythm through *experiencing* it in music, movement, art, and speech. Unless rhythm is experienced through participation, verbalization will produce little significant musical growth.

Learning about rhythm in music, however, should not stop short of understanding its organization and its written symbols. Rhythm scores are a natural outcome of rhythm-oriented activities, when these are planned in a developmental program. As children are guided to feel pattern and pulse in movement, they become ready to see related notation (see page 39). Speech patterns which are reproduced on instruments can be transformed into rhythm scores (see pages 46 and 47). Patterns and phrases created for percussion compositions, to which the balance of this chapter is devoted, need to be written down to be remembered. Such activities generate genuine needs for children to understand the written language of rhythm.

Exploring Rhythm Through Percussion

The American composer-conductor, Howard Hanson, has referred to the percussion family of instruments as the "salt and pepper of the orchestra."

What an appropriate term to describe their importance, not only to a symphony orchestra, but also to music education! This seasoning, when used tastefully, can provide a stimulus for classroom learning with almost limitless possibilities.

Dr. Hanson might have gone even further than "salt and pepper" to include a variety of seasonings and spices, for with the percussion family it is possible to create a multitude of different sound qualities which can be mixed to suit individual taste. Students who have been encouraged to explore the percussive sound possibilities in themselves, in objects found in their environments, and in instruments, as described in Chapter 1, should be able to extend their use of percussion with great imagination and exciting results.

Percussion instruments provide for the classroom a unique medium for creating rhythm compositions. (See Chapter 4 for further discussion of percussion composition.) Through such endeavors students can, in ways fascinating to them, develop and reinforce concepts of musical form, rhythm, tempo, dynamics, and tone color without the confusion of considering melodic and harmonic problems.

Approaches to Percussion Composition

The composer's art is a highly complex science. Let us always be certain that we distinguish between the spontaneous, unskilled, experimental efforts of children and adults and the highly developed art of the composer, lest anyone mistakenly assume that significant musical composition is the result of a hit-or-miss process.

In the broad sense of the term, however, the composition of music begins with, and is based upon, some elemental principles. The child who spontaneously sings

Up and up my roc - ket goes

is creating or making up a melody to tell a story. Another who repeatedly taps

as he walks past a stone wall is expressing a feeling or an idea in rhythm. He is composing in the broadest sense of the term, just as a five-year-old is painting when he splashes bright colors on a piece of newsprint.

The topics of sound exploration (Chapter 1), twentieth-century music

(Chapter 4), and percussion composition are inextricably bound together. As students discover the vast variety of sounds they can create, and as they use these sounds to "orchestrate" rhythm patterns that they develop, they are on their way to percussion composition.

In the early grades beginnings will be as elemental as observing the line notation of a skipping rhythm,

seeing a picture of the woodpecker's song as played on a wood block,

or writing a drum accompaniment to a favorite Indian song:

The simple patterns developed by our six- and seven-year-old drummers, when put into notation, became a rhythm score:

It is important that children have numerous experiences of this type in order to become increasingly familiar with the written language of music—the symbols used to record what is played, sung, or heard.

Starting with Percussion Accompaniments. Percussion accompaniments that students develop for songs they have learned often are recorded in score form. These later can be isolated from the songs and used as the basis for a variety of composing experiences.

Many songs for which percussion accompaniment is appropriate contain rhythmic patterns that can easily be extracted and played on various

An accompaniment to a Latin American song may be the beginning of a percussion composition.

instruments. Students may be helped to play these patterns by thinking or saying quietly the words that belong to their particular excerpt of the melodic rhythm. A good example is found in the version of "Sambalele" that follows.

The patterns suggested at the bottom of page 52 and the top of page 53 are intended to be played as ostinatos throughout the song. These patterns, and similar ones from other songs, may also be used for introductions, codas, and interludes between stanzas of the songs they accompany. Usually it is wise to start one pattern at a time, as an introduction to the song, so that each instrumentalist will have his part well in mind before the singing begins.

"Baizhan Boy" and "Rise and Stretch" (pages 54 and 55) are two other songs that are suitable for percussion accompaniment. Possibilities for utilizing such accompaniments as bases for percussion composition will be developed presently.

SAMBALELE

BRAZILIAN FOLK TUNE
ADAPTED BY M.V.M.

1. Oh, what a boy is Sam - ba - le - le,
2. Oh, what a boy is Sam - ba - le - le,

Nev - er will work, but al - ways play; _____
Nev - er will work, but al - ways play; _____

He climbs the tall pa - pa - ya tree, _____
He rides his bur - ro down the hill, _____

Then like a fish swims in the sea. Oh!
When bur - ro stops he takes a spill. Oh!

Sing and dance and play, Sam - ba - le - le, Hear the mu - sic

say, "Sam - ba - le - le," Sing and dance and play, Sam - ba - le - le,

This is your hap - pi - est day. O - lê!

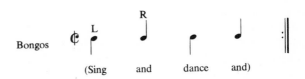

Bongos

(Sing and dance and)

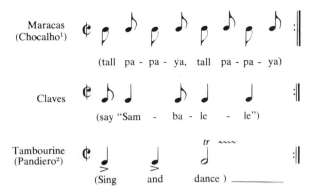

Starting with Clapping Games. Clapping games provide another approach to percussion composition. They are fun for students, and although they may be considered noncreative in the early stages, they can sustain interest, provide continuous challenge, and sharpen mental and physical response to rhythm.

The first games may be purely imitative, in which the teacher claps a pattern in a particular set (or grouping of beats) and the students imitate the pattern without losing a beat.

For example:

The teacher continues to clap in the same set, varying the note pattern each time.

For example: or

This simple game can help children to recognize sets through learning to feel accent. The difficulty of the game may be increased by lengthening the pattern to include two or more patterns or phrases using the same set.

For example:

[1] Pronounced *show-kahl,-yoh;* a single rattle used in Brazil; A gourd rattle or a single maraca can be used, instead of a pair. A long tube filled with small pebbles is also appropriate.

[2] Pronounced *pang-day'-roh.*

RISE AND STRETCH [3]

AFRICAN WORK CHANT

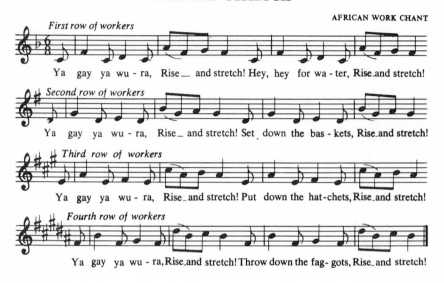

Ya gay ya wu - ra, Rise— and stretch! Hey, hey for wa - ter, Rise and stretch!

Ya gay ya wu - ra, Rise— and stretch! Set down the bas - kets, Rise and stretch!

Ya gay ya wu - ra, Rise and stretch! Put down the hat-chets, Rise and stretch!

Ya gay ya wu - ra, Rise and stretch! Throw down the fag- gots, Rise and stretch!

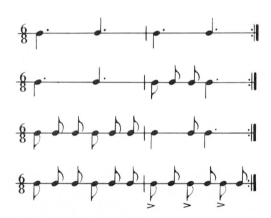

Scored for drums of different pitches.

[3] From *Echoes of Africa In Folk Songs of the Americas* by Beatrice Landeck. Published by David McKay Company, Inc., 1961 and 1969. Used by permission of the author.

BAIZHAN BOY [4]

TUNE FROM THE VIRGIN ISLANDS
WORDS ADAPTED BY ROBERTA MCLAUGHLIN

Bai - zhan Boy, ___ go back _ to your born - in' coun - try, ___

Small is - land boy, ___ go back _ to your born - in' coun - try. ___

You come to my house and eat - a ___ my food,

And leave this ___ old man in a ver - y bad mood; ___

Bai - zhan Boy, ___ go back _ to your born - in' coun - try. ___

Bongos

Claves

Maracas

Quiro

Cowbell

Only on measures 4, 8, and 12.

---

[4] From the album *Latin American Folk Songs* produced by Bowmar Records, Inc. Used by permission.

A greater challenge is provided when the teacher or a child claps a pattern, establishing a certain set, and passes it on from one individual to the next without losing a beat. Each person attempts to clap a pattern that has not yet been used. One fifth grade class clapped fifteen patterns in "4" before a repetition was detected. Such a game requires much concentration, and is even more fun when each person continues to clap his pattern after initiating it. The rhythmic texture becomes increasingly complex as each new pattern is added. Another plan is to divide the class into two, three, or four groups, with each clapping a pattern suggested by a person in that group. Variations of the above ideas are innumerable and include the substitution of instruments for clapping, as well as the use of "built-in" sounds (discussed in Chapter 1).

As children become adept at developing a variety of patterns within sets or two, three, and combinations thereof, they should be helped to put some of them into notation.

"What set was Robert clapping?" asked the teacher of the fourth grade.

"Three," answered several students.

"Yes," continued the teacher. "His accent helped you feel that you should count "*One,* two three, *One,* two, three," and the teacher wrote on the board:

| | | | | | | | |

"What symbol often is used to separate sets?"

"The bar line," said Lucy.

The teacher suggested, "This time, let's use quarter notes for the three beats of equal length," and he wrote,

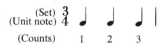

"Now, please clap your pattern again, Robert," requested the teacher. "How many claps were there on the count 'One?'"

"One."

"On count 'two?'"

"Two."

"Were they equal in length, or was one of them longer than the other?" asked the teacher.

After a moment's thought, everyone agreed that they were equal.

"What kind of notes will we need, then, for count 'two'—two notes which will equal one quarter note?"

"Eighth notes."

And thus the discussion continued as the following was written:

When students begin to follow this sequence of thinking in relation to the division of the *whole set into parts,* the process of writing notation takes on concrete meaning, and important concepts regarding the organization of duration are developed. And, when such notation is orchestrated and extended into a musical form, enthusiasm is difficult to contain.

The preceding discussion has centered around patterns of rhythm which are based upon *normal accent.* However, children of all ages should clap and play *syncopated* patterns as well, especially if the patterns are related to a song in which syncopation occurs. A snycopated pattern is one in which the accent falls on a normally weak beat or portion of a beat. Although students undoubtedly will be able to analyze and write normally accented patterns before syncopated ones, they should be encouraged to create and use both kinds of rhythm. Children who have experienced syncopation through many kinds of music activities will be much more ready to understand its symbolization than those who are unable to feel the displaced accent. Snycopation is discussed in detail in Chapter 4.

Percussion Composition Takes Shape. These three patterns were developed by a fourth grade class for drum, tambourine, and finger cymbals, as an accompaniment to the song, "Boom Dali Da."

The patterns were written down after many clapping games, such as those discussed above. The same patterns could have been created for finger snapping, toe tapping, and side slapping. In either case, the resultant score would be suitable for further treatment by the students who created it.

"Let's use this score in a new way today," suggested the teacher. "Instead of playing or clapping the three patterns at the same time, what could we do with them?"

"We could do one at a time," offered Raul.

"Maybe we could do the last one first, and the middle one next, and the first one last," said Rena.

BOOM DALI DA [5]

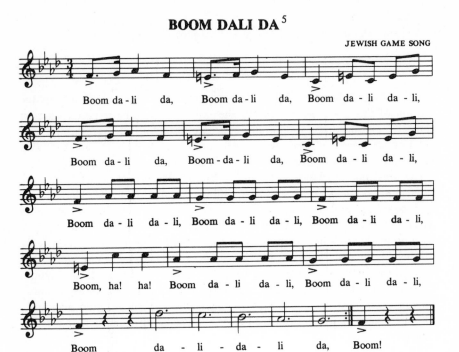

JEWISH GAME SONG

"Good ideas," encouraged the teacher. "Does one of the songs we sang earlier today give anyone another idea?"

"If we started at different times, it might be kind of like 'Music Alone Shall Live,'" responded Raul a bit dubiously.

"Yeah—like a *round*!" sputtered Lyle.

"Let's try the first idea, clapping the patterns as a single piece, and then we'll do it as a round," suggested the teacher.

"That was neat! It makes a good round," said Lyle enthusiastically.

"Now, let's try it with instruments," continued the teacher. "What instruments shall we choose for our orchestration, in order to have some variety in tone color?"

[5] From *Jewish Center Songster*, published by the National Jewish Welfare Board, New York, N. Y. Used by permission.

"We could use drums first."

"Then some ringing ones, maybe, like finger cymbals?"

"The sand blocks would be good, too."

"Good suggestions," replied the teacher. "We'll try the round in that order. The drums will enter first; then after two measures, finger cymbals enter, from the beginning; and finally, the sand blocks. This time, we'll repeat the entire score."

Following the performance of the round, Bruce said, "That was *great*! Couldn't we add some bells with the finger cymbals, or some maracas with the sand blocks? I could play either one!"

The *round* may be thought of as both a simple form of music and a compositional device, that of *imitation*. Students can use the device easily because of its familiarity in songs. The accompaniments on pages 52-55 could be treated as was the example just cited. The patterns could be clapped or played consecutively in unison, and then the entire section used imitatively.

Such rhythm patterns also can be used as *ostinatos* (oft-repeated patterns), over which a rhythm improvisation or a predetermined theme is played. For example, the accompaniment to "Sambalele" might be used as follows:

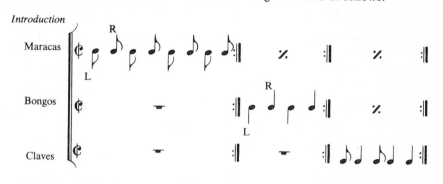

Introduction

Maracas

Bongos

Claves

Ostinatos would then be continued throughout an improvisation on selected original instruments, oriental temple blocks, or melody bells. Following the improvisation, the coda would be played.

Coda

Mar.

Bon.

Cl.

Extending a Simple Beginning. From a similar starting point a group of elementary teachers in a workshop developed a more extended composition for percussion. They began with the following four patterns:

First these were clapped simultaneously by four sections within the class. Next the phrases were used as a round, with each group clapping the four patterns in succession, after staggering their entrances.

The class decided to orchestrate the rhythm composition as shown below:

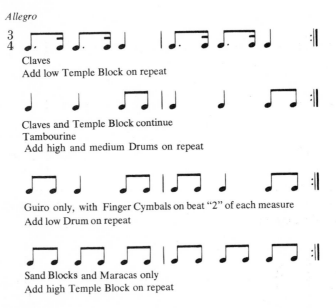

Allegro

Claves
Add low Temple Block on repeat

Claves and Temple Block continue
Tambourine
Add high and medium Drums on repeat

Guiro only, with Finger Cymbals on beat "2" of each measure
Add low Drum on repeat

Sand Blocks and Maracas only
Add high Temple Block on repeat

The phrases were played consecutively, using this instrumentation, and the effect was so exciting to the participants that they deemed the composition worthy of being extended. This was a partial necessity because of its unfinished feeling owing to the eighth notes in the last measure. The group decided to write a contrasting section that would be slower than the first. For additional variety the meter was changed to $\frac{4}{4}$, and as can be seen from the example below, section "B" was more linear than "A."

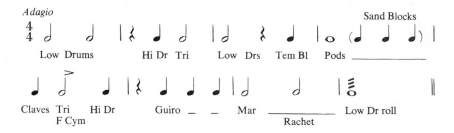

Section "B" was so well liked, and seemed to "end so soon" that someone suggested repeating it. Another member with more knowledge of music than most in the group made the suggestion that a $\frac{3}{4}$ pattern from section "A" be played as a counter-rhythm against the $\frac{4}{4}$ of "B" on the repeat. She chose to play

on a high temple block. The resultant polyrhythm proved most effective, as it added variety and at the same time helped unify the work.

To complete the composition it was decided to return to "A," but this time to play it as a round. The $\frac{3}{4}$ temple block pattern (shown above) proved especially useful, for it was continued for two extra measures after the conclusion of "B," serving as a bridge between the $\frac{4}{4}$ and $\frac{3}{4}$ sections.

The composition *still* sounded unfinished for want of a cadence. A reason for the invention of the coda now seemed obvious to all. The group utilized it as follows:

The effectiveness of the completed composition is difficult to appreciate without hearing it played. The experience was exciting to performers and audience alike, for all had had a part in creating it.

The completed composition is as follows:

(A) *Allegro*

Claves
Add low Temple Block on repeat

Claves and Temple Block continue
Tambourine
Add high and medium Drums on repeat

Guiro only, with Finger Cymbals on beat "2" of each measure
Add low Drum on repeat

Sand Blocks and Maracas only
Add high Temple Block on repeat

(B) *Adagio*

Sand Blocks

Low Drums   Hi Dr Tri   Low Drs   Tem Bl   Pods

Claves Tri   Hi Dr   Guiro — — —   Mar _____ Low Dr roll
        F Cym   Rachet

(B') Add to B, simultaneously:

(Repeat to end of B)

Claves

(Bridge)

Claves continue

(A) Play A as a Round, using same instrumentation

(Coda)

High   Claves   F Cym   Guiro
Drum   Tambourine (struck)
                                            Temple Block

As a result of these comparatively simple first-hand experiences in composing, many teachers in the class for the first time began to understand:

Note values
Measure and bar line
Repeat sign (: ‖)
$\frac{3}{4}$ and $\frac{4}{4}$ meters
Polyrhythm
Uses of unfamiliar percussion instruments
Unity and variety in composition
Imitative form
ABA form (and a variant—ABB'A')
Cadence
Bridge
Coda
Allegro
Adagio

They had begun to explore a new avenue. For some, meanings were still hazy, because of limited music background or old fears about music. But here for all, if they would but open it, stood a door to discovery for themselves and for the children they would teach.

Understanding Musical Form Through Percussion Composition

The preceding examples of beginning rhythm composition have shown the utilization of two short forms of music—the round and the three-part, or ternary (ABA) form. These forms, and others, take on genuine meaning for students who meet them in a variety of situations, through listening, moving, singing, and playing what they have created.

Children need first to recognize likenesses and differences in phrases of songs they sing and in sections of compositions they hear. As they grow in understanding that all composition is based upon the principles of unity and variety, or repetition and contrast, they will discover some of the many ways in which a composer can change a given theme or section of a composition. Even a rhythm "theme" can be altered in the following ways:

Change tempo (play faster or slower).
Change dynamics (play louder or softer).
Change instrumentation.
Use augmentation (make all notes proportionately longer;
   for example, twice as long).
Use diminution (opposite of augmentation).
Substitute rests for some notes.
Change natural accents (may result in syncopation).

Students will enjoy experimenting to see how many variations they can create for a rhythm phrase or theme. A composition in theme and variation form could thus be created from nearly any percussion score.

Forms of music which are particularly usable for beginning percussion composition are the following:

Round and canon.
Three-part, or ternary (ABA), and variants of it.
Rondo.[6]
Theme and variations.

Adjuncts of musical form which can be used readily in percussion composition are introductions, codas, interludes and bridges. In addition, certain compositional devices prove exceedingly valuable for exploration. These include imitation and ostinato, which are discussed also in Chapters 3 and 4. In addition, percussion composition helps free children to express themselves musically through improvisation.

One additional merit of rhythm composition should be stressed. This has to do with its value in providing for individual differences. The student who is able to create or play only a pattern as simple as

or a three-note introduction on a wood block can be as important to the total group effort as one who can execute a difficult syncopated pattern. On the other hand an individual with much ability and creative potential can find a challenging outlet for his interests. Individual needs and abilities often can be met effectively in upper elementary and junior high grades by dividing the class into smaller working groups to create various parts of a composition, after its general framework has been established. Regardless of the method of

---

[6] An example of a percussion rondo created by students is given in Part B.

Meaningful involvement in music may occur as students orchestrate and play their original percussion scores.

production, however, whether by individuals, small groups, or the total class, the creation and performance of percussion composition offers success which is within the reach of all.

CONCEPTS RELATED TO CHAPTER 2

1. There are many kinds of rhythm.
   a. Rhythm can be heard, felt, and seen.
   b. Rhythm can be expressed through sound, movement, and visual materials.
   c. Some characteristics of rhythm are common to all of the arts.
2. All music moves in time and is based upon a rhythmic structure.

3. Rhythm in music is the organization of the duration of sounds and silences.
  a. There is a steady, underlying *pulse* that recurs throughout each piece of music.
  b. Recurring pulses are often referred to as *beats.*
  c. Some beats are stronger than others; this emphasis, or stress, is called *accent.*
4. The measurement of beats in music is called *meter.*
  a. Accent serves to group (or measure) undifferentiated beats into sets of two and three and combinations of those sets.
  b. Accented beats normally appear as the first in a set; in notation, the strong beat normally occurs immediately after a bar line and is the first beat in a measure.
  c. *Syncopation* occurs when accents are placed on beats or portions of beats which are normally unaccented; in syncopation, the accent is said to be *displaced.*
5. A rhythmic *pattern* is a specific combination of long and short sounds and silences.
  a. A rhythmic pattern may be the same as the metric pattern, or it may be different.
  b. Innumerable patterns are possible within a given meter.
6. Rhythm compositions can be created by combining simple patterns in many ways.
7. Repetition and contrast are fundamental principles of composition.

FOR YOUR EXPLORATION

With Movement—Encourage students to:

- Express the feeling of music freely and in an individual way.
- Describe music in terms of its inherent musical meaning. rather than with programmatic, extramusical associations.
- Move to music to express its quality or character.
- Portray structural relationships within the music, for example, rhythmic pulse and pattern.
- Organize movement to show external forms of music.

With Art—Encourage students to:

- Show rhythmic aspects of music through various uses of line.
- Capture musical mood with color and design.
- Portray rhythmic pulse and pattern visually.

With Speech—Encourage students to:

• Listen for natural pattern and accent in words.
• Play the rhythmic patterns of words and phrases on percussion instruments, using names, chants, and poetry.
• Show word patterns in movement.

With Percussion Instruments—Encourage students to:

• Create percussion accompaniments to songs.
• Develop patterns and phrases from clapping games.
• Write selected patterns using blank notation and music notation.
• Discover rhythmic sets (groupings) through clapping and playing percussion instruments.
• Use rhythm patterns as ostinatos over which improvisation is carried on.
• Organize original rhythm scores into simple forms (for example: rounds and canons, two-part, three-part, rondo, and theme and variation).
• Orchestrate original scores with percussion instruments.

With Recordings* mentioned in this chapter:

Bach, Johann Sebastian, "Arioso" from *Cantata No. 156* (on *Bach by Ormandy*, Columbia ML 5065).
Bach, Johann Sebastian, "Badinere" from *Suite No. 2 in B Minor* (on *Adventures in Music*, Gd. 3, Vol. 1, RCA Victor).
Bartok, Bela, "Bear Dance" from *Hungarian Sketches* (on *Adventures in Music*, Gd. 3, Vol. 2, RCA Victor).
Chabrier, Emmanuel, *España* (on *Adventures in Music*, Gd. 5, Vol. 1, RCA Victor).
Debussy, Claude, "Jimbo's Lullaby" from *Children's Corner Suite* (on *Concert Matinee*, Bowmar Orchestral Library, BOL 63).
Debussy, Claude, "Nuage" ("Clouds") from *Nocturnes* (Angel 35977).
Grieg, Edvard, "In the Hall of the Mountain King" from *Peer Gynt Suite No. 1* (on *Legends in Music*, Bowmar Orchestral Library BOL 59).
Griffes, Charles, *Clouds* (Mercury 50085).
Hanson, Howard, "Children's Dance" from *Merrymount Suite* (on *Adventures in Music*, Gd. 3, Vol. 1, RCA Victor).
Ravel, Maurice, "Laideronette, Imperatice des Pagodes" ("Laideronette, Empress of the Pagodas") from *Mother Goose Suite* (on *Fairy Tales in Music*, Bowmar Orchestral Library, BOL 57).

*Because of the rapidity of change in availability of commercial recordings it is suggested that a catalog or a record dealer be consulted before ordering recordings listed here.

Rogers, Bernard, "Dance with Pennons" from *Three Japanese Dances* (Mercury 90173).

Shostakovitch, Dmitri, "Polka" from *Age of Gold* (Ballet Suite) (Victor VIC 1184; Westminster 18293).

Stravinsky, Igor, "Danse Russe" from *Petrouchka* (Columbia MS 6332; London 6554).

Vaughan Williams, Ralph, *Fantasia on Greensleeves* (on *Adventures in Music*, Gd. 6, Vol. 2, RCA Victor; Westminster 14111).

Chapter 3

Exploring Pitch—Discovering
Melody and Harmony

Melody-making is one of the joys of childhood. Children's dramatic play often is accompanied by their humming and singing to themselves and others. Although the young child's resources for creating melody—his command of pitch and rhythm—may be limited and unrefined, the spontaneous song-expression of a child has a magic all its own.

As children grow from babyhood, they move from nondescript gurglings and cooings to singing more distinct intervals of pitch. There is research that seems to indicate that the interval of a descending minor third,

is universally used in children's chant, even in cultures not exposed to modern media of communication. Young children's exploration of pitch should *not* be limited to this particular interval, however, or to any specific tones or organization of tones. In fact, such limitation to any one kind of interval or scale may inhibit children's musical creativity, as well as their growth in aural acceptance of music from many cultures and periods. Children who are encouraged to explore pitch more *freely* may accidentally discover intervals and scales which are utilized in a wide variety of folk and composed music. The original tunes of these youngsters will have a freshness not found in melodies created by children who are limited to the minor third interval, pentatonic scales, or even diatonic scales.

Fostering Spontaneous Song Expression

The success of children's melody-making will be directly related to their attitude toward singing. Free and spontaneous singing is natural to children, unless they have been conditioned otherwise. There is little time, space, or

When you accidentally play a familiar tune by ear, everyone listens.

encouragement these days for children to enjoy *making their own songs.* Living for most is hurried, crowded, and filled with admonitions to be quiet. Thus the school may be the only place a youngster may find freedom to sing about his airplane, his pet rabbit, or his friend. How much more he will enjoy the song if it is one he has created!

The kindergarten teacher who hears a child singing during play may note on paper the words he sings, and later use his song fragment as a springboard for creating a group song.

"Tommy, I heard you singing about your bunny while you were playing today. The words of your song were, 'This is the way my bunny hops' and you were hopping as you sang it. Could you sing it for the whole class to hear?"

Although Tommy may not sing the same tune again, the praise for his expression at play probably will encourage him to try. He may sing a different tune, or, indeed, he may sing his words to the tune of a familiar song without realizing it:

This is the way my bun - ny hops,

If this happens to be the case and another child mentions it, the teacher might suggest adding some words to Tommy's and finishing the song in a way that is different from the familiar song:

He hops and flops, He flops and stops.

Spontaneity may also be encouraged by challenging students of any age to complete the melody to a song they do not know. For young children a single phrase might be used:

Oh, say, are you hap - py? Yes, Yes, Yes!

For older students more complete songs are interesting to finish:

DANCE SONG

FLEMISH FOLK TUNE

Come, and let us go danc - ing, go danc - ing, go danc - ing,

Come, and let us go danc - ing Go danc - ing all a - round.

As children gain confidence in singing extemporaneously, they may enjoy seeing how many different endings they can create for a given unfinished song.

Singing conversation can prove valuable in helping young children grow in their perception of melodic movement and in freedom to create melodies. The teacher may sing a question instead of speaking it, and a child may respond by singing also:

Repeat with same tune or a different one.

How ma - ny child- ren are   ab - sent to - day?   Two   children are absent today.

The resourceful teacher will find many ways of adapting the ideas above to a wide variety of classroom activities.

Sing a Story

The primary classroom was filled with charts of original songs, such as those below. Many of the tunes contained only two tones, and some had no indication of time value. Each one, however, could be sung or played by its creator.

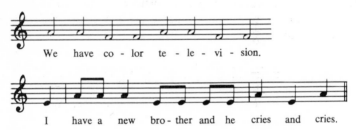

We   have   co - lor   te - le - vi - sion.

I   have a   new   bro - ther and   he   cries   and   cries.

The teacher had stimulated high interest in melody-making by allowing two children each morning to *sing a story*. The two individuals were named on the previous day, so that they could have a one-sentence story ready when they arrived at school the following morning. No one ever forgot!

The initial musical task of each child involved was to choose two resonator bells on which to play his tune. He was allowed to come to the room a few minutes before school began if he wished to do so. After he had chosen his bells and tried out different ways of using them to fit his sentence-story, he was asked to sing his story to the class; then the class joined him. Sometimes it was necessary for the teacher to put the words on the board or on a strip chart before a child could sing his words and tune together. The teacher kept a pile of one-staff tagboard strips and a felt pen handy.

Although at midyear some younger members of the class still had difficulty in singing on pitch, tremendous growth had been seen in the development of this skill as children's original tunes were sung on various occasions by the entire class and by the individuals who created them. By the end of the year each child could sing his stories with amazing accuracy.

"Billy and Cynthia," said the teacher, "you are our melody-makers today. Do you have your stories ready?"

"I do," offered Cynthia. "My story is about where I went yesterday. I went to the zoo and saw the tigers."

"What a fine story," encouraged the teacher, writing the words on a strip chart under a blank staff. "What bells have you chosen for your tune?"

Looking at the letter names imprinted on the bells, Cynthia replied, "I have F sharp and C sharp." After a few tries Cynthia played and sang:

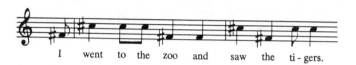

I went to the zoo and saw the ti - gers.

"Good for you, Cynthia. Let's all sing Cynthia's song," suggested the teacher, as she wrote the notes above the words on the chart.

"Now, Billy, it's your turn."

Billy, much more shy than Cynthia, showed his bells, which were low C# and D#. "I want to sing about the thunder last night," he said somewhat timidly.

"A good idea," replied the teacher warmly. "I wondered whether anyone would choose to sing about the surprise storm we had. What did the thunder do, Billy?"

"It roared like a lion," offered Billy, undoubtedly influenced by Cynthia's zoo story.

The teacher was surprised and pleased at Billy's burst of expression, for this was his first imaginative story since he had entered the class late in the semester. The words, "The thunder roared like a lion" were put on a chart.

"Now what will your tune be, Billy?" asked the teacher.

The child hesitated, and so the teacher suggested he play the two tones several times for the class to hear. This seemed to free him, and after a pause, he played:

The thun - der roared like a li - on.

"Oh, that's a very good tune, Billy. Let's all sing it several times."

After the class had enjoyed this "song," the teacher made a suggestion. "You know, we might say some other things about the storm and make a longer song."

The group was enthusiastic about the idea, as was Billy, so the language arts period was spent writing one-sentence stories about lightning, rain, and wind.

On subsequent days three of these were chosen to finish the song. Then tunes were added, using a variety of pitches, and the following group song resulted:

OH, WHAT A STORM!

The teacher had challenged the class to make their tunes interesting through questions such as:

"When you see a streak of lightning, does it look high in the sky or low?"
"Was the sound of the wind high or low? Loud or soft?"
"Did the rain fall up or down? Were the drops big or little? How could you make a melody sound like *great big* drops of rain?"

Thus six- and seven-year-olds were learning to make a melody meaningful to a text through use of:

- High and low pitches.
- Descending melodic movement.
- Long and short tones.
- Loud and soft dynamics.

Singing Commercials—Past and Present

sang Jimmy, a seven-year-old whose assignment it was to announce the lunch hour to the class.

The second grade had been learning about some of the many ways people have used songs to communicate with each other. The teacher had found the story of the New England town crier a strong incentive for learning to tell time and for helping develop vocal freedom and melodic sensitivity. The child who was appointed Town Crier for the day could create his own tune to announce the time at 9:00 A.M., noon, and 2:40 P.M., and at any other times requested by the teacher.

The children had become equally fascinated with vending calls. They had first learned some traditional ones as they studied about markets and food distribution, and then had become enthusiastic about creating their own calls. Nearly every day someone had a new "commercial" to sing for the class.

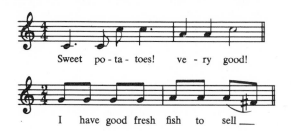

The calls became so original that the teacher decided to put them in a booklet. Rather than take the time each day to write them as the children sang, she recorded them on tape and once a week entered them in the class book. In this way children could hear themselves sing, which delighted them, and the teacher could see that all members of the group had an opportunity to contribute. Children were encouraged to try to play their vending song tunes on the bells in order to *see* as well as *hear* how the melodies moved. They could observe the wide leap in the "sweet potato" call as the C to C octave was played and seen on the staff. By contrast the fish vending song used tones that were close together. Thus the children's own creative endeavors involving their ears, eyes, and hands, were bringing meaning to the term *melody*.

What Is a Melody?

The question, "What is a melody?" elicits a wide variety of responses, many of which are more subjective than scientific. The reply often includes qualifying adjectives such as *pleasing, beautiful,* and *harmonious.* These words do not define, or even describe *melody* per se, but reflect the judgment of an individual about a given tune or kind of tune. A Strauss waltz, which might be considered a beautiful melody by a European, might be completely distasteful to someone reared in India or Bali. The latter reaction would result from the individual's aural orientation to music based upon scale systems vastly different from those of Johann Strauss and the Western world.

An objective definition of a melody might be "a succession of tones that move in time and express a musical idea." This indicates that a melody is comprised of two components, namely, pitch and duration. The tones of a melody may be taken from any of a number of systems of pitch organization. Such systems usually are called *scales,* and usually the pitches bear a particular relationship to a tonal center.

The most familiar systems of pitch organization are built of whole steps and half steps, and are as follows:

> 7 tone—*major* and *minor* diatonic (5 whole steps and 2 half steps).
>
> 7 tone- *church modes* (also diatonic; these include major and minor systems).
>
> 5 tone—*pentatonic* (tonal—no half steps; semitonal—1 or 2 half steps).
>
> 12 tone—*chromatic* (12 half steps).
>
> 12 tone—*"row"* (no tonal center).

Much of the exotic music of the world is based upon *microtonal* scales, that is, various divisions of the octave into intervals smaller than half steps. Such music may sound out-of-tune to the individual oriented to whole-step—half-step music.

Throughout a child's school experience there should be opportunities for him to hear, sing, play, and create music based upon a variety of pitch systems. Certain kinds of scales, however, seem to lend themselves to youngsters' early explorations because of their lack of harmonic implication.

Making Music with Pentatonic Scales

The term *pentatonic* refers to a five-tone scale. Although this might be any arrangement of any five tones, certain five-tone organizations have been used more commonly than others. The two which are most familiar are (1) a five-tone scale containing no half steps, sometimes referred to as a *tonal penta-scale;* and (2) a five-tone scale containing two half steps, called a *semitonal penta-scale.*[1] It is interesting to note that the latter scale in descending form was prevalent in ancient Greek music. It is also possible to find many examples of music based upon a pentatonic scale containing one half step only.

Tonal penta-scale   Semitonal penta-scales

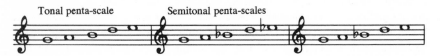

[1] From *Harvard Dictionary of Music* by Willi Apel (Harvard University Press, Cambridge, Mass.).

Perhaps the easiest, although not necessarily the most interesting pentatonic scale for children's experimentation is the tonal penta-scale containing no half steps. This scale lends itself to improvisation and simple composition because no half step dissonance can occur, regardless of the tones which are played simultaneously. The lack of dissonance in music based upon the tonal penta-scale creates a feeling of tranquility. Such music often is said to have an Oriental quality, because much music from Asia utilizes this system of pitch organization. The very lack of dissonance, however, can also cause such pentatonic music to become monotonous—one of many reasons for not limiting children's exploration to this particular scale.

The black keys of the piano offer a good starting point for children to create with tonal penta-scales. A song such as the following may provide motivation:

PLEASE TELL ME

Words and Music by MVM

1. Lit - tle night owl, tell me, with your big brown eyes so wide,

How you see in dark - ness what I can - not see!

2. Little cricket, tell me, Does your singing make you tired?
   Do you not get weary, Singing just one song?

3. Humming bird, please tell me How you stand in air so still,
   Sipping lotus blossoms, Nectar oh so sweet!

An accompaniment to this song might be developed with ostinatos (repeated motifs or patterns) played on any of the black keys of the piano or comparable tuned bells. Ostinatos are most effective when their rhythms are simple.

For example:

Other appropriate instruments for accompaniment include finger cymbals, wood blocks or Oriental temple blocks, light rattles, and gong. An accompaniment with introduction and coda, such as the example shown on the following page, is quite effective with "Please Tell Me."

It is important to move away from the black keys for variety, and to avoid the misconception that they constitute *the* pentatonic scale. Tonal penta-scales (built of three whole steps and a step-and-a-half) should be constructed beginning on many pitches, as should semitonal penta-scales. Songs based upon both kinds of scales can be found in many textbook series, although semitonal examples are not plentiful. One well-known song based upon a pentatonic scale containing two half steps is "Sakura," often called "Cherry Blooms" or "Cherry Blossoms."

Setting Haiku to Music

One of the most exciting activities carried on in the fourth-fifth grade during the year had been the writing of Haiku poetry. The students had found

*Pentatonic scales lend themselves to impro-
visation and musical settings of Haiku.*

it easy and satisfying to create poems using this Japanese form of expression, which consists of three lines containing five, seven, and five syllables respectively. The teacher had observed a great measure of growth in the children's vocabulary of descriptive words, as description is the heart of Haiku. Haiku usually deals with nature, and complete sentences are seldom found. The form is intended simply to project a reflection upon life.

"If you were to set one of these poems to music, what kind of a scale would you choose," asked the teacher.

Children at first discussed various major and minor key possibilities. Then someone remembered the pentatonic scales with which they had worked earlier in the year. "Wouldn't a pentatonic scale be good for a Japanese poem?" he questioned. "A lot of Japanese music has just five tones."

The class quickly agreed. And so they decided to choose a pentatonic scale with which they could use their Oriental temple blocks. The teacher some months before had labeled these as B, D, E, F#, and G#. The students had played them to accompany several Oriental songs. They recalled that they could be used to best advantage with two pentatonic scales—D, E, F#, (A), B, and E, F#, G#, B, (C#). Either of these tonal penta-scales would allow for the inclusion of four temple blocks. This set of five, unfortunately, did not constitute one of the more commonly used pentatonic scales.

The first-mentioned scale was selected for the Haiku setting. One member of the class was asked to pick all the D's, E's, F#'s, A's, and B's out of a twenty-bell set of resonator bells. Then a low B (below middle C) that was available was added. A student was asked to play the bells in ascending and descending order several times:

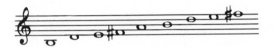

"Let's take a look at the Haiku you've chosen for a musical setting," suggested the teacher, and the group read together:

Fiercely blow, cold wind,
    Icy blasts will harm us not,
Spring will come again.

"Which line is the most active and powerful?" the teacher asked.
There was agreement that it was the first.
"How could we make the music for these words very strong?"
The students considered the possibilities of using accents, long tones, low or high pitches, and a slow tempo. With these ideas in mind they tried several tunes and finally decided upon:

Fierce - ly blow,— cold wind,

It was decided that the next line should start on a high pitch as a contrast to the first phrase. For rhythmic variety two eighth notes were used on one syllable in each measure:

I - cy blasts will harm us — not,

"Is the third phrase of this Haiku one of finality or of expectation?" challenged the teacher, to emphasize the importance of suiting the music to the meaning of the text. The class quickly caught the idea and discussed possible ways of giving the setting a feeling of anticipation. They decided that the line should move upward and should end on an unexpected tone:

Spring will come a - gain.

"That's a neat ending," said an enthusiastic boy who hitherto had been somewhat unimpressed with the whole undertaking.

"Let's add some instruments, like we used with pentatonic scales before," suggested another.

"But not too many," cautioned the first, "because it might spoil the neat song."

It was decided that the arrangement would begin in true Oriental fashion—with the sound of the gong. Many possibilities were then explored for resonator bell ostinatos. Several were chosen:

"We ought to use the xylophone; it sounds real Oriental," said a girl, and she began to experiment with patterns. She soon played one that the group accepted:

"I could make a wind sound on the song bells, like this," said another girl excitedly as she played an ascending glissando on the third beat of the second measure.

"What about the temple blocks?" reminded a boy, who obviously wanted to play them. After considerable experimentation, it was decided that a special melody should be written for the temple blocks, as there were already enough ostinatos. The temple block part which was developed frequently doubled the tones of the melody:

"Let's put it all together," encouraged the teacher, as she began to list on the board the order of entrances of the various instrumental parts.

When the first performance was completed, there was much enthusiasm. However, the boy who had described the song as "neat" was disturbed. "There are too many instruments," he complained. "You can hardly hear the song."

On the second performance the high resonator bell ostinato was omitted and all remaining instruments were played more softly. This time everyone seemed satisfied. From very simple raw materials and limited experience a delicately beautiful piece of music had been fashioned:

The following are examples of original Haiku created and set to music during summer workshops for teachers. They are included to illustrate the variety possible when this poetic form is set pentatonically.

Pentatonic Scale

Finger Cymbals

Alto Metallophone

Voices

Soft __ sil - ken pe - tals __

Soft   pe - tals

Bloom, but on - ly   for a - while. Pale, tran- sient beau - ty.

Bloom   on - ly   for a - while, Pale, tran - sient beau - ty.

Pentatonic Scale

Introduction
Gong   *Bass Xylophone   *Alto Metallophone

Voices   (Melody)   Finger Cymbal

Oo _____   Night   wind   whis - per - ing,

F. Cym.

Moon - light _____   and   sil - ver   wa - ter,

Gong - p ⌐ 3 ⌐   *Coda* 4 meas. of Ostinatos   Gong

Shi - ver - ing cat - tails.

Pentatonic Scale:

*Repeat throughout composition.

84

Understanding Musical Form Through Pentatonic Composition

Pentatonic scales are as useful for the creation of instrumental compositions as they are for tunes to accompany children's texts. Through compositions of their own students may come to better understand the simple forms of music. These forms take on concrete meaning when they have been exployed for original pieces of music, and then are discovered in standard compositions that children hear.

Pentatonic composition may be begun in a variety of ways, one of which is through the isolation of an accompaniment to a song. An example may be seen on page 78. This accompaniment, or a similar one, may be used as the foundation for a pentatonic melody that the entire class writes. Such a melody can be built, a phrase at a time, as various students try out their ideas on bells or piano. Pitch contour and rhythmic interest should be considered as the melody is constructed. The previously created accompaniment, consisting mainly of ostinatos, may then be added.

Another way to develop a melody is to have each student write a short pentatonic phrase and then combine several of these phrases into a melody. Here again, pitch contour and rhythmic interest should be taken into account as the phrases are selected, to assure a balanced melodic structure. For example:

When such a melody is played with a previously created accompaniment, the resultant composition can be quite effective and satisfying to children. Although short, the material provides a beginning for a composition of greater length. Possibilities for extending the composition include:

- Adding a contrasting section, to create a two-part (**AB** or **AABB**) composition.
- Repeating the first section following the contrasting section, to create a three-part (**ABA** or **AABA**) composition.
- Adding an introduction, coda, and interludes or bridges.
- Creating a theme and variation form by changing the first theme in any of a number of ways (for example, playing the theme in retrograde—backwards; changing the meter; changing the melody instrument(s); playing the melody in imitation—as a canon).
- Adding two or more contrasting sections to create some rondo form (for example, **ABACABA**, **ABACADA**).

"Chinese Dance" is a students' pentatonic composition in AABA form, with introduction and coda:

CHINESE DANCE

It should be stressed at this point that one of the greatest benefits to students of such *composing* is the growth of their appreciation for the task of the serious composer. Thus, it is essential for children to recognize that, although they may be working with music in some of the same ways as mature composers do, they are experimenting, and that true *composition* is a highly refined art and skill. This point may be emphasized by providing for frequent listening to compositions related to students' work. For example, when boys and girls are creating ostinatos for pentatonic or percussion accompaniment, they might hear "Ostinatos" from *Tabuh Tabuhan* by Colin McPhee, or *Ostinatos* by Henry Cowell. Listening related to children's work with pentatonic scales might include the first of *Three Japanese Dances* by Bernard Rogers, other portions of *Tabuh Tabuhan,* and authentic gamelon music of Bali and Java. Hearing selections such as these should help develop a feeling for the kind of music being emphasized, and also build an appreciation for the skill that is required to create such music.

Many of the activities suggested for use with pentatonic scales may be adapted to whole tone (hexatonic) scales. These, like the tonal penta-scale, contain no half steps, and thus they permit improvisation and composition without chance of minor second dissonance. The two possible forms of the whole tone scale are as follows:

Compositions for related listening include "Voiles" from *Preludes,* Book I, by Debussy, "Mists" from *For the First Time* by Hanson, and "Whole Tone Scale" from *Mikrokosmos,* Book V (No. 136), by Bartok.

Creating with Diatonic Scales

Attempts at song creation such as those described at the beginning of this chapter may grow from the use of a few tones to experiments with many kinds of scales, including the most familiar diatonic. The term *diatonic scale* refers to any seven tone organization of pitches which contains five whole steps and two half steps. The bulk of composed music until the late nineteenth century was based upon diatonic scales, and thus it is inevitable that children will experience more music of this type than any other. As boys and girls create music from diatonic scales, the question arises as to how they can be helped to obtain interesting rather than trite results. The ecclesiastical modes offer one possibility.

The term *mode* is used most broadly to denote any kind of pitch organization that provides the raw material for a composition. Thus, it is possible to speak of the major mode, the minor mode, a pentatonic mode, or a hexatonic mode. The scale systems of the Eastern world, including India and the Orient, also are sometimes referred to as *modes*. More specifically, the term mode is used with reference to the church or ecclesiastical modes which dominated Western music until the sixteenth century. The authentic church modes, which are diatonic scales, are formed by using only the white keys of the piano, and are named as follows:

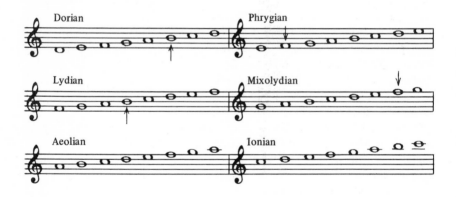

Upon examination, it will be seen that the ionian mode is what is now called the major scale, and that the aeolian is the natural minor. Only one tone in each of the other four modes distinguishes it from a major or natural minor form. In the dorian, the raised sixth degree (B) keeps the scale from being a natural minor. The phrygian mode is characterized by the lowered second degree (F). The lydian and mixolydian are differentiated from major scales by the raised fourth (B) and the lowered seventh (F) degrees, respectively. Therefore, melodies which are modal in feeling emphasize these characteristic tones; otherwise, the character of the melody is major or minor.

Any of the modes can be constructed in any of twelve forms, or transpositions, by beginning on any of the twelve chromatic tones and retaining the intervallic pattern of the mode. For example:

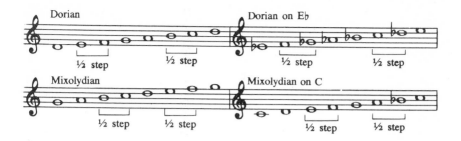

When the modes are used for children's creative endeavors, it may be wise to concentrate upon the white key forms to avoid confusion.

Making Modal Music

The third grade had experienced a fascinating trip to the harbor. They had been escorted through a large freighter, had examined a small tugboat, and had viewed an old sailing vessel. They had visited a cannery, and had commented freely on the odors, as well as the sounds around them. They had spent time watching and listening to the ocean, the sea gulls, and the various kinds of buoys. For many, this was a first experience at the seashore.

Desiring to capture the children's impressions and enthusiasm, as well as to reinforce their new-found knowledge, the teacher provided for them to paint and write about their experiences when they returned to the classroom. The visual and auditory aspects of the trip were emphasized in the discussion which preceded the creative writing, in an attempt to help the children write descriptively. Many of the stories which resulted were typical third-grade accounts of what had been seen and done. Others, however, took on a more poetic form, and some were truly creative. For example:

> The waves pound against the sides of the old ship.
> The big waves splash and run up on the sand.
> Listen to the splashing, pounding waves!

The teacher decided to use this poem as the text for an original class song. On the day following the writing she said, "Your poems and stories were so interesting that I thought you might like to write a tune for one of them. I had a hard time choosing, but this one almost seemed to sing itself. Listen to it, and see whether you can hear a tune in your mind."

She read the poem, and then played up and down the white key bells which she had removed from the larger set of resonator bells. The pitches she had selected were D up an octave and a third to F:

The class read the poem several times to gain a feeling for its rhythmic flow, and they talked about which words were held the longest, and which were shorter.

"Let's have three or four people come up and play a short tune on these bells, just to get some ideas for a melody," suggested the teacher. Several children did so. When one girl played a few tones which seemed to have possibilities, the teacher said, "I wonder whether Irene's tune would work with the first few words of the poem. Can you make your tune move like the beginning of the poem, Irene?" And the teacher read, "The waves —— pound —— a-gainst the sides."

With a bit of help, Irene said the words and played,

"Let's sing that much, and then ask someone to sing the rest of the phrase for us," said the teacher. And so, by playing and singing in this fashion the song was created. As patterns were developed on the bells, the teacher asked the children to tell her the names of the tones they were playing, and she wrote the notes on the staff. When "The Sea" was finished, she completed the rhythm. Later, after the song was familiar to the class, sound effects were added with drums, sand blocks, and rattles.

THE SEA

The waves pound a - gainst the sides of the old ship.

The big waves splash and run up on the sand.

List - en to the splash - ing, pound - ing waves!

An analysis of this song reveals that it utilizes the phrygian mode. The tonal center seems to be E, with the many F's giving the modal flavor. Other modes, such as dorian or lydian, might have resulted, or a major or minor feeling might have prevailed, depending upon which tones had been emphasized. The middle C was purposely omitted from the selection of bells to minimize the possibility of a song in C major. Although these third grade children did not know they were using one of the modes, their musical experience was broadened by creating and singing a song based upon a scale other than a traditional major or minor. At another time the selection of bells might contain only one octave, to further limit the possibilities to a modal setting.

All classes may not be as accepting of modal sound as the third grade just described. Older students who have not had opportunities in the lower grades to sing, hear, and create with modes other than ionian (major) and aeolian (minor) may find it difficult to accept a dorian, phrygian, lydian, or mixolydian flavor.

The teacher of a seventh grade music class decided to give her students the opportunity to become acquainted with the modes in conjunction with a unit on melody in music. She briefly explained that there was a time when all Western world melodies were based upon the church modes. She then played the modes on the white keys of the piano, after asking the students to listen for the two scales that sounded most familiar. The major and minor were easily identified. Next, the class was asked to write some original poetry that could be set to music, hopefully by using the modes. Students worked in groups of three to write poems about themselves, their school, nature, or something with which they were well-acquainted. When the poems were completed, the teacher suggested using the dorian mode to create melodic settings. Each group was given the dorian tones (D to D above) from a set of resonator bells.

The results of this endeavor were totally disappointing. No melodies were finished. Some students were so disturbed by the lowered seventh in the scale that they went to the bell cases and replaced the C♮ with a C#. The teacher concluded that she had not adequately prepared or motivated the class, and therefore decided to try for a group melody during the following session. Several of the more promising poems were read to the class, and the following one was selected to be set to a melody:

The Rise and Fall of the Butterfly

The butterfly is a graceful thing,
Going up and down with painted wing;
  When he lands on a flow'r
  He never finds it sour.
But when he lands on a Venus flytrap—
That's the end of his fluttering flap!

To promote a modal melody, the teacher again played the dorian scale, and suggested that someone try to sing a tune for the first line of the poem. The students seemed reluctant to do this, and so the teacher played several melodic ideas for the first line and asked the class to select one. This they did, with a few students volunteering ideas regarding the changing of certain intervals. This procedure was followed for the first half of the song—through the word "flow'r." As the period ended, the teacher asked for volunteers to take a copy of the partially completed song home in order to finish it; five students did so.

The first portion of the song had been written on the board with no bar lines, and the five volunteers were asked to return the completed song with meter and measures, as well as pitches. Although the class had worked rather extensively with rhythm notation and percussion composition earlier in the semester, the finished songs were turned in *without meter and bar lines*. The melodies were presented to the class, and one was selected to be learned. Its rhythmic organization was determined by the students as they read the poem and marked bar lines before the syllables with the strongest accents. It then became obvious that not all measures contained the same number of beats, and that changing meter would be required.

THE RISE AND FALL OF THE BUTTERFLY

SEVENTH GRADE CLASS

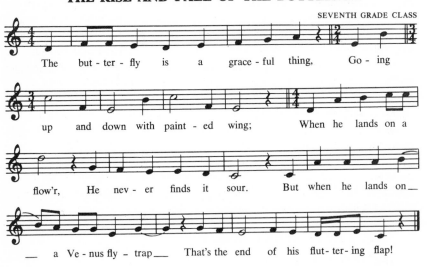

An observation of the completed song reveals that the first half of the melody, which was originated by the teacher with some changes made by the class, is *modal* in feeling. The last half, created by a student, immediately

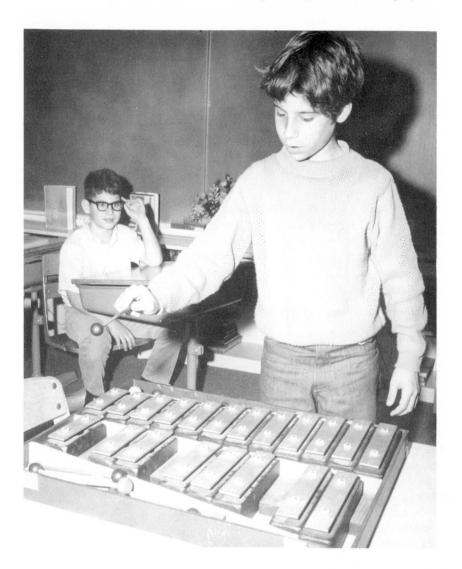

Children need varied opportunities to improvise and to create their own melodies.

shifts to a *C major tonality*. This was the case with all five of the melodies submitted. The results of this experiment led the teacher to the following conclusions:

1. Students need to sing and hear modal music before they can be expected to find satisfaction in creating it.
2. Opportunities should be provided for students to improvise and create many kinds of melodies by working both in small groups and as a total class.
3. Original verse could be prepared in English classes, with the music teacher and the English teacher working toward common objectives. This would allow more time for motivating creative writing suitable for a musical setting, and music time would be conserved for work with music per se.

General implications from this account seem to be that students at all levels need much more experience in singing and hearing melodies having tonalities other than major and minor, and that all children need many and varied opportunities to improvise and create melody.

Discovering Thematic Variation

One of the first lessons to be learned by any composition student deals with the two underlying principles of musical form, namely, *unity* and *variety.* These also are referred to as *repetition* and *contrast,* for unity is achieved by means of the former, and variety through the latter. Exact repetition is easy to detect, as is the sharp contrast created by the introduction of completely new musical material. More subtle, however, is that contrast achieved by altering existing material. There are numerous variation devices that composers use to develop a musical idea, and in so doing, achieve unity and variety at the same time.

Students can develop concepts related to balance in musical structure through creating and analyzing their own compositions. Boys and girls can easily understand the need for repetition to make a piece of music whole or complete, and for contrast to keep music from becoming monotonous. They may recognize that a percussion piece which uses only one pattern of rhythm lacks interest, or that a pentatonic composition needs to return to its first theme to seem complete. It should be relatively easy for students to use repetition and contrast in these ways. Possibilities for achieving *thematic variation,* however, will need to be explored.

Some kinds of variation can be utilized by children more easily than others. Although elementary and middle or junior high students may be introduced to a number of variation devices through listening to music, they will lack the skill necessary to incorporate all of these into their own compositions. Students at these levels may be able to achieve variation in their creative musical endeavors through the following means:

Change of timbre (instruments).
Change of register (octave).
Change of meter.
Change of mode or of key.
Change of tempo.
Change of dynamics.
Alteration of tones in a melody.
Alteration of rhythm pattern.
Use of imitation (in percussion, especially).

The extent to which students can use variation in their compositions will depend upon their previous musical experience and understanding. Some possibilities for achieving variety are suggested in the discussion of percussion composition in Chapter 2 and pentatonic composition in Chapter 3, and in examples throughout Chapter 4 and Part B. The account that follows presents one approach to the subject of thematic variation.

The fifth grade class had just sung "Yankee Doodle" and had accompanied it with Autoharp and drums. The teacher said, "Pretend that you are a composer and that you have decided to write a short patriotic piece in which you want to use 'Yankee Doodle' as a main theme. If you repeat it too many times in its original form, it will become quite monotonous. What could you do to make it more interesting?"
At first everyone looked puzzled. Then, after some thought, several of the children recalled listening to "Variations on 'Pop Goes the Weasel'" by Cailliet, several months earlier.
"You could change the time," suggested Freddy.
"What do you mean by 'time'?" questioned the teacher.
"Well, like from march time to waltz time," answered Freddy, undaunted.
"You certainly could change the time, or the meter," encouraged the teacher, as he wrote the word *meter* on the board. "Let's try it."
With some help at the beginning, the class sang "Yankee Doodle" in waltz time:

"What else could you do to make this tune sound different?"
"Could we do it in minor and make it sad?" asked Sylvia, dubiously.
"We could put it in a minor key," replied the teacher, "but that wouldn't necessarily make it sad. Let's try it in the minor mode, but use the original meter and tempo."

The class thought these two variations were great fun.

"Could we add another drum?" offered a percussion enthusiast.

"Or other instruments?"

Ideas were coming quickly now.

"We could change it by singing it slower," suggested Lucille, as she remembered the Cailliet variations.

"Or softer!" boomed out George in a heavy voice.

"Good. We have five possibilities for creating contrast," responded the teacher, and he read the list from the board:

Change meter.
Change mode (major-minor).
Change instruments.
Vary tempo.
Vary dynamics.

The teacher explained that the last two didn't actually change the melody, but that they were important means of achieving contrast. He then asked whether the class could think of any other possibilities. None was volunteered, and so he continued, "An American composer named Virgil Thomson did choose 'Yankee Doodle' as the basis for a short composition. Listen the first time to see whether Mr. Thomson used any of the changes on your list. You may discover some variation devices that you didn't include."

As the class listened to *Fugue and Chorale on a Yankee Doodle Theme* their faces showed that they recognized the familiar tune, but also that they were unsure of what was happening in the music. During the discussion which followed, some children said they thought they had heard "Yankee Doodle" in a minor key, and all were sure that the tune was played by different instruments. Other comments reflected the observation that "Yankee Doodle" never was played in its entirety; in fact, only the first eight tones were heard. Students also discovered that there was a lot of music "that wasn't 'Yankee Doodle'."

"What happened when different instruments played the 'Yankee Doodle' theme?" asked the teacher, and he played the first part of the recording again.

"Each instrument that comes in plays it, like a round," said Paula.

"Yes, each instrument *imitates* what the instrument before it has played. Imitation is one important way of creating variation in a melody," said the teacher. "Did anyone notice whether the second instrument came in on the same pitch as the first?"

Most of the class thought it had. The teacher suggested that the children hum with the first instrument and listen for the entrance of the second. When this was done, it was obvious to most of the children that the pitch of the second instrument was different from that of the first. The term *fugue* was presented and explained simply, as was *chorale,* and the selection was studied further on subsequent days.

Other examples chosen to illustrate thematic variation were Stravinsky's "Greeting Prelude," "Desert Water Hole" from *Death Valley Suite* by Grofe, and *American Salute* by Morton Gould. Attention was focused upon the variation devices used in each selection.

The teacher decided to find out how successfully fifth grade students could create variations on a tune familiar to them. He divided the class into four groups with eight or nine students in each, and asked each group to create one variation of "Shoo Fly." Some of the possibilities for melodic variation were recalled from previous discussions. The teacher offered to assist any group that needed help in implementing their plans. Fifteen minutes were given to the project. Two of the groups remained to work in the classroom. One went outside, and the fourth was assigned to an adjacent classroom that was empty for twenty minutes.

Of the four groups, three produced a variation for "Shoo Fly." The fourth spent so much time trying to decide which kind of variation to use that they never had a chance to practice. The three completed variations were as follows:

1. One group wanted to change the meter of the song to $\frac{3}{4}$. Although this required some initial guidance from the teacher, the children were able to continue on their own, and found they count get started easily if one member played an Autoharp introduction in three, and said "ONE, two, three, ONE, two, three." The children sang as follows:

SHOO FLY

Shoo fly, don't both-er me, Shoo fly, don't both-er me,

2. Group two decided upon a change to a minor key. They needed more assistance than the first group. The teacher played the F minor scale, emphasizing the flatted third degree (A♭) as the starting tone for the song. The group then were able to sing the refrain in this minor key.

3. The third group worked quite independently, adding a percussion accompaniment with sand blocks and finger cymbals. They varied the melody by playing the tuned bells and sand blocks instead of singing the words "Shoo fly":

(Bells + Sand blocks)

Throughout the verse (beginning with the words, "I feel, I feel, I feel"), the sand blocks played

with the finger cymbals playing on the word "star" both times it was sung. The arrangement was very effective.

Although these first efforts were quite unpolished, the children who shared them with the rest of the class seemed pleased with their accomplishment. From very rudimentary beginnings such as these, boys and girls may be helped to understand more complex variation devices such as augmentation, diminution, ornamentation, and imitation. At this level the skill that students gain in *using* variation techniques is less important than the motivation toward *understanding* them. Participation in simple processes can pave the way for conceptualizing broader facets of musical composition.

Exploring Traditional Harmony

Children should be exposed to the sounds of many kinds of harmony at an early age so as to gain a broad aural orientation to music. They also should have opportunities to become well-acquainted with the classical system of harmony upon which much of the music they hear is based. Experiments with nontraditional harmonies are discussed in Chapter 4. The suggestions that follow, dealing with traditional triadic harmony, are not presented as new ideas, for they are standard practice with many teachers. They are intended only to reinforce convictions that such experiences are effective means of helping boys and girls of all ages understand the rudiments of the harmonic system underlying many of the songs they sing and much of the music to which they listen.

Young children may first become aware of chordal accompaniment as they strum an Autoharp while the teacher changes chords. Later, one child may press the bars for a one-chord or a two-chord song while another child strums. When a song that is accompanied by the Autoharp or other chording instrument becomes very familiar, the class may be asked to listen (not look) and raise their hands each time they hear a different chord sound. At first this may be difficult, but with practice children of all ages should become able to recognize differences in the sounds of chords, especially if the changes occur regularly. The ability to hear harmony may be encouraged through a music center in the classroom, where a child may quietly strum a chording harp. If

*Exploration may lead to the discovery of en-
semble harmony.*

such a center is well-located, and if standards for its use are developed by the
class and adhered to consistently, the soft sounds that result from such
free-time exploration should not distract those doing other kinds of work.

Tuned resonator bells are invaluable for developing an understanding of the
ways in which chords are created by combining tones. There are a few songs
that can be accompanied with one chord throughout. These offer opportunity
for three children each to play a bell. It may be difficult for young children
to coordinate the striking of three bells simultaneously in rhythm. In this case
a tremolo effect may be obtained by having each child strike his bell as
rapidly and steadily as possible. Older students can accompany two-chord and
three-chord songs in like manner, or by playing with the pulse of the song as
they would strum an Autoharp.

The individual resonator bells had just been brought into the fourth grade.
The set was new, and this was the first class to use it. These students had not
worked with this instrument in the lower grades, as this was a school that had
very limited equipment. Thus, there was great excitement when the bells
arrived. The teacher explained that each bell had been properly tuned, and
that this instrument, like any other, should be used with care. One student

was asked to experiment with a mallet and one bell to discover the playing technique required. It was observed by all that the mallet had to be lifted quickly in order for the sound to resonate. Each student then had a chance to come to the bells and play four or five tones to get the feel of the instrument.

On subsequent days the bells became important in several ways. A simple descant was played on them. An introduction was added to a familiar song. One bell was used for "chimes" in a song, and glissando sound effects were discovered.

"Instead of using the Autoharp to accompany 'Sandy Land' today, I thought we might try the bells. How could we use them?" challenged the teacher.

"We could play the descant instead of singing it," suggested Kim.

"Yes, we could. Is there any other kind of accompaniment which would be similar to the Autoharp accompaniment," asked the teacher. "What do we play on the Autoharp?"

"We play G and D_7" replied Jim proudly.

"Right," said the teacher, smiling, "but what are G and D_7?"

"Chords?" responded Jim with a questioning tone.

"How could we play chords on the bells?" continued the teacher.

"By playing some of them together," replied a piano student.

"Let's see which bells we'd need to use for 'Sandy Land'," said the teacher, as she began to write on the board. "These are the tones of the G major scale, in which 'Sandy Land' is written in your books. We'll make a human scale," and she handed the eight bells—G to the G above— to eight children. "Stand here in a row, and let's see how your scale sounds."

After the scale had been played up and down, the teacher continued, "You've said the G and D_7 chords are needed for this song. What is the bottom note in the G chord?"

Phyllis said hesitantly, "Would it be G?"

"It certainly would," replied the teacher. "That's the reason it's called a G chord—because G is its base, or 'root.' Will the person who is playing G please step forward. Now, the kinds of chords needed for this song are built by using every other note in the scale. There will be two other tones in the G chord. Will the two people who think they belong in the G chord please step out and join Jill."

With a little prodding from their friends, the two children holding B and D stepped forward to join G, and the chord was played several times. Building the D_7 chord in like manner required adding F#, E, and D to the scale below G, in order to have enough bells to complete the chord. The teacher explained that the chords with a "7" in them needed an additional tone. When the two chords were completed, the teacher gave both groups a chance to play their chords a number of times in rhythm:

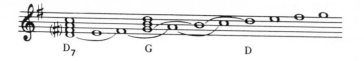

The teacher said, "Now we'll see whether the people playing the bells know when to change the chords while the rest of us sing 'Sandy Land'." An introduction was given by playing the G chord four times, and the class began to sing. At first there was much confusion and giggling, as some of the children played at the wrong times and then stopped playing. With an admonition to listen and think, the second attempt showed much improvement, and the third rendition was perfect except for two players in the D_7 chord who forgot to stop when the chord changed to G on the last word of the song.

Subsequently the accompaniment to "Sandy Land" was transposed to the key of F by the same process as was described, so as to help the class gain a concept of movable "do" and see the relationship of the chords G-D_7 to F-C_7. Gradually concepts were built regarding the relationships of the I, IV, and V_7 chords in all keys. This active involvement in chord building developed an understanding of simple triadic harmony in a more vital way than any amount of discussion alone could have done.

Building chords as described in the preceding example will lead to the discovery of tones that are common to two or more chords. The fact that the *fifth degree* of the scale appears in both the I and V_7 chords is useful in the creation of simple descants or countermelodies, which can be played or sung with familiar songs. Such an activity grew out of a discussion of two different types of vocal arrangements that a sixth grade class had been singing.

Two of the favorite songs of the sixth grade students were "Las Mañanitas" and the arrangement of "Cindy" shown on page 102.

One day after both songs had been sung, the teacher said, "Both of these songs are arranged in two parts, and yet they are quite different. In what ways are they different?"

First responses related primarily to the differences in subject matter of the texts. The teacher stressed the idea of the ways in which the tones were combined to create two-part arrangements.

Jamie said, "Well, in 'Las Mañanitas' we're all singing all the time, and in 'Cindy' the descant rests part of the time."

"Yes," replied the teacher, "in 'Las Mañanitas' both parts are singing the same words, and the same rhythm, but different tones. In 'Cindy' the two parts are singing different words and different rhythms, as well as different tones. This is the reason for calling the part sung above the melody a *descant*. This part is really a second melody, or a *countermelody*."

The word *texture* was introduced, and *harmonic* (chordal) texture was compared with *contrapuntal* (melody against melody) texture by singing and listening to representative musical examples.

LAS MAÑANITAS

CINDY [2]

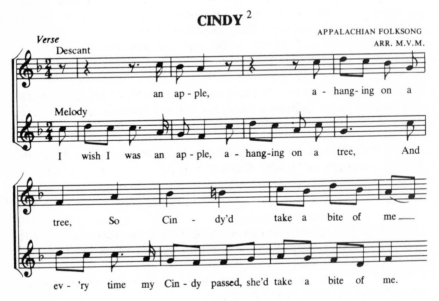

At another time the teacher asked, "Does the Autoharp produce a contrapuntal or a harmonic texture?"

"Harmonic, because it makes chords," volunteered Butch.

"Then how come we can play the Autoharp when we sing 'Cindy'?" scoffed Pete.

"An excellent question," replied the teacher, encouraged with Pete's evidence of understanding.

After some discussion regarding the requirements for a contrapuntal arrangement, it was concluded that harmonic considerations are usually the basis for combining tones, even when the texture is contrapuntal.

"Maybe we could create a countermelody to a familiar two-chord song," suggested the teacher. "How about 'Are You Sleeping?' for a first attempt? What chords do we use to accompany this song, and what would be the tone which is common to both of them?"

After a bit of figuring, the answer came that the chords were G and D_7, and that the common tone was D. It was recognized that, because this tone was in both chords, it would sound all right throughout the song. Some of the students then sang

Wake up, John! Wake up, John!

as an introduction, and as a countermelody while the rest of the class sang the melody.

A more complete descant was developed for "Down in the Valley." The class analyzed the tones contained in both the F and the C_7 chords used to accompany the song. Then they played the broken chords on resonator bells. Finally they developed words and melodic patterns to serve as a countermelody to the original melody, as shown on page 104.

There are many possibilities for pitch exploration that have not been included here for lack of space. Additional ideas are presented in Chapter 4. As children create melodies from two or three pitches or from many kinds of scales, as they alter familiar or original melodies by various means, and as they combine pitches to produce a variety of harmonies and textures, they will grow in understanding not only the organization of pitch, but the general structure of music as well. It is impossible to consider pitch organization without being concerned also with rhythm, timbre, dynamics, and tempo. Thus it is imperative that music always be approached as an expressive whole, and that any study of its parts be related to the total discipline.

DOWN IN THE VALLEY

AMERICAN FOLK SONG

CONCEPTS RELATED TO CHAPTER 3

1. Tones are arranged sequentially to create melody.
   a. Every melody has a pitch contour or shape.
   b. Every melody has a rhythmic structure or organization.
   c. A song is a text set to melody; a well-constructed song has a melody
      that reflects the meaning of the text.

2. Melodies usually are based on some system of pitch organization called a *scale.*
   a. There are many systems of pitch organization.
   b. The most familiar system in the Western world is the diatonic scale, a division of the octave into seven tones of half-step and whole-step intervals.
   c. Much music of the world is based upon pentatonic scales, divisions of the octave into five tones.
3. All music is based upon the compositional principles of unity and variety.
   a. Unity is achieved through repetition.
   b. There are innumerable possibilities for creating contrast, through many kinds of melodic, rhythmic, and harmonic variation.
4. Tones are combined vertically to produce harmony.
   a. It is possible to harmonize a given melody in many ways.
   b. The most familiar kind of Western world harmony is based upon triads.
5. The texture of a composition is determined in part by the way in which pitches are combined.
   a. Harmonic (homophonic) texture is achieved through the use of consecutive chords.
   b. Contrapuntal (polyphonic) texture is achieved by combining melodic lines.

FOR YOUR EXPLORATION

With Pitch—Encourage students to:

•Sing spontaneously.
•Finish incomplete phrases and songs with original tunes.
•Sing answers to questions that are sung.
•Make up tunes, with or without words, using two or three tones.
•Think of the meaning of words as they are set to music.
•Listen to music based on many scale systems.

With Pentatonic Scales—Encourage students to:

•Improvise freely using the black keys of the piano or bells.
•Create melodies from pentatonic scales, using both tonal and semitonal penta-scales; improvise accompaniments to these.
•Develop pentatonic ostinatos as accompaniments to songs.
•Set Haiku to music based upon pentatonic or whole tone scales.
•Create larger pentatonic compositions using various forms of music.

With Diatonic Scales—Encourage students to:

•Listen to the sound of the church modes, by playing them on the white keys of piano or bells.
•Build modal melodies as settings for creative writing.
•Identify variation devices used by composers in music that is heard.
•Try various means of altering familiar melodies to create variations.

With Traditional Harmony—Encourage students to:

•Listen to familiar tunes harmonized in more than one way.
•Indicate when chords change in Autoharp accompaniments.
•Build I, IV, and V₇ chords on resonator bells, to accompany songs.
•Transpose I, IV, and V₇ chords on Autoharps and bells.
•Create countermelodies based on common tones in accompanying chords.
•Distinguish between chordal and contrapuntal textures.

With Recordings* mentioned in this chapter:

Bartok, Bela, "Whole Tone Scale" from *Mikrokosmos,* Bk. V (No. 136), (Vox SVBX 5425, 3-record album).

Cailliet, Lucien, "Variations on Pop Goes the Weasel" (on *Adventures in Music,* Gd. 4, Vol. 1; and *Music, USA,* Bowmar Orchestral Library BOL 65).

Cowell, Henry, "Ostinato Pianissimo" (on *Concert Percussion,* Time 8000).

Debussy, Claude, "Voiles" from *Preludes,* Bk. I (Mercury 90391).

Exotic Sounds of Bali (Gamelon music) (Columbia MS 6445).

Gould, Morton, "American Salute" (on *Adventures in Music,* Gd. 5, Vol. 1, RCA Victor).

Hanson, Howard, "Mists" from *For the First Time* (on *The Composer and His Orchestra,* Vol III, Mercury MG 50357).

McPhee, Colin, "Ostinatos" from *Tabuh Tabuhan* (Mercury MG 50103).

Musical Memories of Bali (London International TW 91308).

Rogers, Bernard, *Three Japanese Dances* (Mercury MG 50173).

Stravinski, Igor, "Greeting Prelude" (on *Stravinksy Conducts Favorite Short Pieces,* Columbia CML 6048 or CMS 6648).

Thomson, Virgil, "Fugue and Chorale on a Yankee Doodle Theme" (on *Music, USA,* Bowmar Orchestral Library BOL 65).

---

*Because of the rapidity of change in availability of commercial recordings it is suggested that a catalog or a record dealer be consulted before ordering recordings listed above.

Chapter 4

Making Contemporary Music Meaningful

"...All impartial musicians and music lovers were in complete agreement that never was anything written in music so incoherent, shrill, muddled and utterly shocking to the ear."

"... is a hideous, incomprehensible jargon of noise, cacophony, and eccentricity, musically valueless and only interesting to ears that prefer confusion to meaning."

"... *First Piano Concerto,* like the first pancake, is a flop."[1]

Are these reactions to the works of twentieth century composers such as Charles Ives, Igor Stravinsky, or John Cage? Indeed, not! The first comment was written in 1806 in reference to a performance of the "Overture" to Beethoven's opera, *Fidelio.* The second was published in the Boston *Gazette* in 1887, and the work criticized was Lizst's "Mephisto Waltz." The "flop" referred to in the third excerpt was Tchaikovsky's.

Nevertheless, similar comments might be found in tomorrow's newspaper—words written to express disapproval of sounds unpleasing to the ears of the listener. Although man always has with him both the old and the new, he tends to like and accept that which is familiar. This position of musical comfort is found by a majority of adults today in works of the Romantic era (roughly, the nineteenth century), for this is the music that they have heard most frequently. Much less familiar, and consequently less palatable to many, is music often described as new, although its evolution has been taking place for over half a century.

Contemporary music refers primarily to music of the twentieth century, though not all music written during this century is in the contemporary idiom. This period is one in which unusually strong breaks with tradition have come about. It is a time in which composers have gone in myriad directions in

[1] See *Lexicon of Musical Invective* by Nicolas Slonimsky, for similar quotations.

search of new musical freedom. Some of the results have been stark and startling.

Open-mindedness is essential if we are to hear what this newer music has to say. This is not meant to imply that all that is new should be considered good or that the open-minded listener will automatically like contemporary music or even accept it intellectually. It does mean that the desire to find out what a piece has to offer, combined with some knowledgeable basis for listening will develop the ability within the listener to make choices and, in time, to discriminate between music that has intrinsic worth and music that does not.

Within the space of this chapter it is not possible to lay a solid foundation for the understanding of contemporary music. It is hoped, however, that the reader will become sufficiently intrigued by the ideas discussed herein that he will search out ways of increasing his own understanding of music in this idiom, and of developing similar interests in the students with whom he works.

Contemporary Music—for Children?

Chapter 1 stressed the teacher's responsibility to open children's ears to the world of sound. The "sound world" within which today's children are living is one containing rhythms, harmonies, and timbres not common to the sound orientation of many adults. These newer sounds are woven into the musical scores of television and motion picture productions. Musical commercials often employ them. They belong to this century, this decade, this day. Consequently, the young child may accept the "Circus Music" from *The Red Pony Suite* by Aaron Copland more readily than he does the "March of the Toys" by Victor Herbert. The first piece contains nontraditional melodic progressions, changes of meter, tone-cluster harmony, and polytonality, whereas the latter reflects traditional nineteenth century uses of the components of music.

Twentieth century music offers some unique avenues for children's creative endeavors. Much that has been presented in the first three chapters of this book relates directly to the use of contemporary music with children and youth. Ideas previously suggested for the exploration of rhythm, melody, harmony, and environmental sound are extended in this chapter to apply specifically to newer music. Examples include composing with percussion instruments (introduced in Chapter 2), altering familiar melodies through octave displacement and fragmentation (an extension of Chapter 3), and developing tape recorder pieces (another "sound source" related to Chapter 1). Through such activities students can build musical skills with genuine purpose, while developing understandings that enable them to bring meaning to the contemporary music they hear. The order of chapters in this book is *not meant to imply that experience with traditional music should precede contemporary*. The situation is quite the opposite, as was pointed out in the last paragraph. Music representative of various periods and styles should be the fare of even the youngest child, in order to develop his musical perception before preconditioning occurs. This chapter is separated solely for the purpose of calling attention to the importance of contemporary music in the curriculum, and for emphasizing the relationship of contemporary music to the music of the past.

Thus, two points should be kept in mind as this chapter is read. First, contemporary music should *not* be treated as a separate or isolated kind of music, but should be given its rightful place in the total music education of children. Second, the younger the child, the less opportunity he has had to become conditioned to more traditional music or against newer sounds. The younger the child, the more he should be able to approach all sound with open ears and mind. It is essential that children hear, discuss, and move to a great deal of contemporary music throughout the primary grades, before any attempt is made to intellectualize the compositional techniques employed in its creation.

Discovering New Timbres

The third graders were listening with a puzzled look, as the teacher played a recorded selection. They had been asked to try to identify the instruments being used in the music they were hearing. The piece was *Amores No. 1* by John Cage.

After the first hearing of *Amores,* a rather precocious Mark replied that he had heard "piano and gong and wood blocks and xylophone and tambourine." As he had covered all the ideas others had formed, no one wished to add to the list. The class was amazed when the teacher explained that the entire piece had been played on the piano, and that the variety of sounds had been created by "preparing" the piano strings. She then read a few of the directions for placing screws, bolts and nuts, and pieces of rubber between the strings in a prescribed manner to produce the desired results. The teacher emphasized that the children should not try out the idea on home or school pianos, as the success of the project depends upon considerable understanding of the instrument and the music to be performed. It was suggested that the class might experiment later with the Autoharp to obtain similar effects.

A brief discussion about banshees preceded the playing of a second composition bearing the title, *Banshee.* Roger, whose father worked with computers, said, "They must have done that one on an electronic machine." Other members of the class agreed for want of a better idea.

"I heard a few notes that sounded like a piano," offered Marcia. "Maybe the piano was prepared like in the last piece."

"An interesting idea," replied the teacher; "Marcia is right about the

Banshee being a composition for piano, but not 'prepared' piano. Listen to part of the piece again to see how the piano was used."

Hands were raised almost before the music began, as the swishing sounds heard previously were recalled. The children were fascinated by the idea of playing *inside* the piano, and were eager to experiment with the Autoharp to try to produce sounds such as these.

"Composers are always trying to find new ways to play familiar instruments," explained the teacher. "Would you look at the instruments we have in our room, and think of a new way to play some of them to make a different sound."

As the children made suggestions they were asked to try out their ideas. Some were more original than others, but to these eight-year-olds the ideas were unique. Experiments included:

Autoharp—Plucking strings; strumming with different kinds of objects, such as felt, metal, and wood; placing objects between the strings, *à la* John Cage; tapping strings with mallets; tapping the wooden box.
Wood blocks—Tapping with different kinds of beaters.
Tambourine—Striking with mallets as well as hands.
Drums—Striking in various spots including the shell, and with different kinds of mallets; scratching drum heads with fingernails and rubbing with the palms of hands.
Sand blocks—Playing with long smooth strokes, and with short detached movements.

The children were so fascinated by these experiments that the teacher decided to encourage their interest. The following week she again asked them to try to identify the instruments heard, as she played the first portion of *The Wayward* by Harry Partch. Nearly every child felt he could identify some instrument, eight of which are introduced individually in this selection. The children's guesses included "an out-of-tune piano or Autoharp," electric guitar, harp, giant temple blocks, wood blocks, chimes, bongo drums, xylophone, and train whistle. Indeed, there were sounds which might have been made by all these instruments.

"Those were very good guesses," said the teacher, "and it was a rather unfair question to begin with, for Mr. Partch has made his own instruments. Some of them are similar to the instruments you mentioned, but they are tuned differently (based upon 43 pitches to the octave). Here are some pictures of his 'cloud-chamber bowls,' the 'boo' (bamboo marimba), the 'kithara,' and the 'chromelodion.'[2] You see, composers not only use familiar

[2] A booklet containing pictures and descriptions of Harry Partch's instruments accompanies each of his recordings. These are listed in "For Your Exploration" at the end of this chapter.

Original instruments constructed by Danlee Mitchell, percussionist. Mr. Mitchell utilizes these instruments in many of his percussion compositions.

instruments in new ways, as Mr. Cowell and Mr. Cage did, but they often create new instruments that will produce completely new sounds.

"Here is a composition that calls for some original instruments more like the ones in our room than Mr. Partch's. You also will hear some familiar percussion instruments, such as high and low drums, a tambourine, and wood blocks. In addition are an Indian rasp or scratcher, a brake drum, a large metal thundersheet, glass bells, clay bells, cowbells, and wooden bells without clappers, called 'dragons' mouths.' As you listen, try to think about the variety of sounds you hear, and about some object you might find which could be used to make such a sound."

The children were excited about *Canticle No. 1* by Lou Harrison. They talked about the crispness of the gourd rattle sound, the variety of pitches ringing from the different bells, the hollow roar of the "dragons' mouths," the distant roll of the thundersheet, and the light, tinkling contrast of the timbres produced by the glass bells. They discussed the term *canticle* (little song) and now were eager to bring their own instruments with which to create a third grade "Percussion Canticle." (See Chapter 1 for an account of a class experiment with original instruments, and also pages 124-27 of this chapter.)

The possibilities for discovering new sounds and using them creatively are legion and hold a fascination for all, whether five, fifteen, or fifty years of age. The human infant is alert to every change of timbre and dynamic level. It is necessary only to keep alive, or to reawaken this sensitivity, in order for a child or an adult to feel the excitement of discovery that a mature musician experiences when he brings a new sound to the world of music.

Newer Freedom in Rhythm

How many songs can you recall which are written in $\frac{5}{4}$ or $\frac{7}{8}$ meter? How many times have you heard the meter change within a song or symphony? Have you been aware that some music is written with no meter signature? Perhaps all this has taken place without your knowledge of what was happening.

One of the most obvious characteristics of contemporary composition is the departure from traditional uses of rhythm. The *Rite of Spring* (*Le Sacre du Printemps*) by Igor Stravinsky, first performed in 1913, introduced an era in which *rhythm*, rather than melody or harmony, was to become significant as a *unifying factor* in music. In this composition, the driving, usually syncopated rhythms and rapidly changing meters give substance to the composition, despite comparatively static harmonies and sparce melodies. Within this musical score, now over half a century old, can be found examples of nearly all contemporary uses of rhythm. Syncopation, achieved by various means, occurs so consistently as to characterize the rhythm of the entire score. Irregular meters, such as $\frac{5}{16}$, $\frac{7}{4}$, $\frac{9}{8}$ ($\frac{4}{8} + \frac{5}{8}$), are common. These change frequently, even from measure to measure, as shown in the following excerpt from "Danse Sacrale," measures 12-31:

$$\frac{5}{16} \left| \frac{2}{8} \right| \frac{3}{16} \left| \frac{2}{8} \right| \frac{5}{16} \left| \frac{5}{16} \right| \frac{2}{8} \left| \frac{3}{16} \right| \frac{2}{8} \left| \frac{3}{16} \right| \frac{2}{16} \left| \frac{3}{16} \right| \frac{2}{8} \left| \frac{3}{8} \right| \frac{3}{16} \left| \frac{2}{16} \right| \frac{3}{16} \left| \frac{2}{8} \right| \frac{2}{16} \left| \frac{3}{16} \right.$$

The ballet is filled with polyrhythms, that is, the simultaneous use of two or more kinds of rhythm. Such polyrhythm may combine different meters, or unlike patterns of accent within the same meter.

These rhythmic devices—syncopation, irregular meter, changing or shifting meter, and polyrhythm—are found infrequently in pre-contemporary music of the Western world. They are not uncommon, however, in folk music from many parts of the world. Syncopation and complex polyrhythm are indigenous to African music. Syncopation also characterizes much of the music of coastal Latin America and the Carribbean areas which reflect strong African influence. Irregular and shifting meters can be found in much folk music, especially of Balkan and Slavic countries.

The teacher should search out and use much music which employs these rhythmic devices, in order that children of all ages may become free in using them. Boys and girls will learn to feel these rhythms only as they sing them, move to them, play them, and create them.

Syncopation

Limited examples of syncopation can be found in compositions from nearly any period in music history. Not until the twentieth century, however, did syncopation become a dominant force in composed music. Young children are entitled to the pleasure and challenge of singing, hearing, and playing syncopated rhythms before they can analyze them. Older students who have been deprived of these experiences during their primary years often have great difficulty in feeling and participating freely in syncopated music.

It is important that intermediate and upper grade students begin to understand as well as feel syncopation and to identify it in written music. This understanding begins with the ability to recognize *normal accents* in music. Only then is it possible to discover accents that fall on weak beats or portions of beats. It is these *displaced accents* that create syncopation. The following examples show one measure of regular accent followed by one of syncopation:

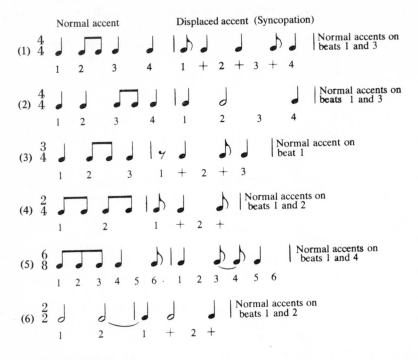

It can be observed in these six examples that syncopation has been created by several means:

- •Placing accent marks (>) on normally weak beats (examples 2, 4, and 5).
- •Changing the rhythm patterns of notes (examples 1 and 3).
- •Tying a weak beat to a strong one that follows (examples 5 and 6).
- •Placing a rest on a normally strong beat, followed by a note on a weak beat (example 3).

The effect of a syncopated rhythm is directly related to the rhythm which precedes it, that which follows it, and that which accompanies it. It is possible to feel *displaced* accent only as it is related to *normal* accent. For example,

if clapped indefinitely by itself will begin to sound like

or normal accent. The syncopation will be strongly evident, however, if the pattern is used in any of the following ways:

Students will have little difficulty in including simple patterns of syncopation in their percussion scores if they have used percussion instruments appropriately to play such patterns in familiar songs. (See Chapter 2, pages 50-54.) The percussion score below was created by a seventh grade class that had been experimenting with syncopation through shifting accent:

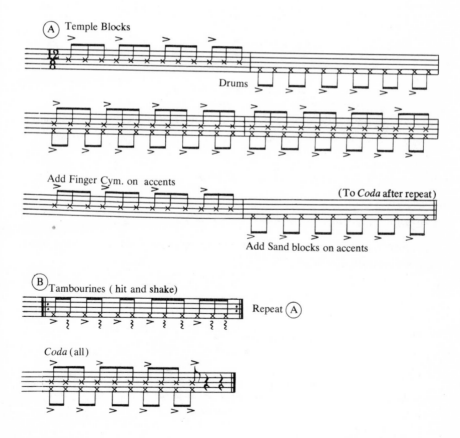

Older students may enjoy the challenge of seeing how many different patterns of syncopation they can develop from a rhythmic idea such as

The most commonly found and easiest to play syncopated pattern is "short, long, short, long, long":

or

This pattern is found in many songs, such as "Mister Banjo," "Sambalele," and "Tinga Layo." From this the true *clave pattern* can be developed easily:

The pattern for claves usually adds a less syncopated measure to emphasize the syncopation of the first measure:

Clave pattern:

Irregular and Shifting Meter

Irregular meters are those created by combining subsets of two and three beats into one measure. For example:

The same effect often can be achieved through the technique of shifting the meter. This may be indicated in the initial meter signature, provided the change is to be regular and continuous:

Or, the composer may mark the changes as they occur:

As pointed out above, much folk music is based upon irregular or shifting meter. In actuality, this music consists simply of long and short tones that follow either a text or a dance pattern. Such music is sung and played quite freely. But when it is set down in Western notation, the result is an irregular meter, such as $\frac{5}{4}$ or $\frac{7}{8}$, or a shifting meter. "The Shepherd Boy" is given as an example:

THE SHEPHERD BOY [3]

GREEK FOLK SONG
TRANSLATION BY ARISTIDES E. PHOUTRIDES (ADAPTED)

1. Once I was a shep-herd boy,_____ I kept my sheep, but __
2. Now I spend my days in sing - ing, I play my flute till the

knew no joy;____ Then one day a ____ maid - en found_ me,__
hills are ring - ing; For one day a ____ maid - en found_ me,__

Charmed me, and __ her bright eyes bound me.__
Charmed me, and __ her bright eyes bound me.__ *Tun - de, tun - de,

tun - de, tun - de!_ Tun - de, tun - de, tun - de tun - de.

*(Toon - day).

[3] From *Botsford Collection of Folksongs, Vol. 3,* by Florence H. Botsford. © Copyright 1933 by G. Schirmer Inc. Used by permission.

A change of meter often is used to accommodate the words of a song. When such songs are sung naturally there is no feeling of irregularity, for the melody follows the natural phrasing of the text. This is illustrated in "The Cuckoo in the Tree" and "Shenandoah."

THE CUCKOO IN THE TREE [4]

GERMAN FOLK SONG

ENGLISH WORDS BY GRETEL DUNSING

1. On yon-der tree a cuc-koo, Sim-sa-la-dim-sa-la-du-sa-la-dim,
   Auf ei-nem Baum ein kuk-kuck,

On yon-der tree a cuc-koo sat.
Auf ei-nem Baum ein kuk-kuck sass.

2. There came a fine young hunter .. bold.   4. But when another year had passed .. by.
3. He shot the poor gray cuckoo ... dead.   5. There was a fine new cuckoo ... there.

SHENANDOAH

SEA CHANTEY

1. Oh, Shen-an-doah, I long to hear you, A-
2. I long to see your smil-ing val-ley, A-

way, you roll-ing riv-er, Oh, Shen-an-doah, I long to
way, you roll-ing riv-er, I long to see your smil-ing

hear you, A-way, I'm bound a-way, 'Cross the wide Mis-sou-ri.
val-ley, A-way, I'm bound a-way, 'Cross the wide Mis-sou-ri.

[4] From *Golden Bridge*, published by the Cooperative Recreation Service, Inc. Copyright 1952 by Lynn Rohrbaugh. Used by permission.

"The Donkey Cart" and the related listening examples discussed below have been used successfully to help upper elementary and junior high students feel, and then analyze irregular meter.

THE DONKEY CART [5]

WORDS BY MARGARET MARKS
GREEK FOLK DANCE

[5] From *Music Around the World,* by James L. Mursell, et al. © 1956, 1962, Silver Burdett Company. Used by permission.

Tac - a - tac - a - tac - a - tac goes the don - key,
Tac - a - tac - a - tac - a - tac goes the don - key,

You don't have to give a whack to the don - key.
In the eve - ning we'll come back with the don - key.

Coda

Drums   Whoa!

The natural accents in "The Donkey Cart" subdivide the beats of each measure into subsets of 3 - 2 - 2:

1   2   3 - 1   2 - 1   2

As students sing, and play the drums as indicated to accompany the song, they will begin to feel this division. The Greek folk song, "The Shepherd Boy" (page 117), uses this same grouping throughout.

The "Unsquare Dance" by Dave Brubeck is an excellent piece for comparative listening. Students may be told that this music also is written in "seven," and asked to discover whether the grouping within this composition is the same as that in "The Donkey Cart." The class will soon recognize that it is impossible to count "1 2 3 - 1 2 - 1 2," because the accents in "Unsquare Dance" divide the measures into groups of 2 - 2 - 3 ("1 2 - 1 2 - 1 2 3").

As a final related listening experience, "Waltz" by William Russell might be played, with students being asked to discover its rhythmic organization. They may be surprised that a composition by this title should be written in "seven." The slow tempo and strong accents of this percussion piece make its metric organization easy to identify. The bass tone clusters that occur on beats *one* and *four* throughout the composition at first create alternating subsets of three and four beats. Near the middle of the piece, however, strong accents occur on the fifth beat, and the feeling shifts to four plus three, despite the continuing pattern of the bass tone clusters. This composition is a favorite with students because of its rhythmic interest and its unusual uses of percussion instruments.

The teacher was clapping various rhythm patterns and the fifth graders were imitating her, as they were accustomed to do. Some of the patterns were rather complex.

"What set am I clapping now?" she asked, as she clapped,

"Three."

"How did you know?"

"Because you accented on *one* and there were two beats between accents."

"Try another," she suggested. "What set is this?" and she clapped,

"That's *two*," came a reply in a tone that indicated disdain for such a simple question.

"What about this one?"—

After a brief hesitation, someone ventured, "That's two, then three, then two—back and forth!"

"How could you write a meter signature for it?" questioned the teacher.

No one knew. Then one small girl took a chance and wrote $\frac{2}{3}$ on the board.

"That was a good try," encouraged the teacher, "but this would mean that there are two notes of what kind in each measure?"

The girl laughingly agreed that this could not be correct, because "there's no third note, only quarters and halves!"

"Can someone put these notes into a measure?" continued the teacher, clapping the pattern again.

When a brave member of the class put

on the board, one of his pals quickly said the signature could be $\frac{5}{4}$, and the set could be *five*.

"Could these sounds be put into measures in any other way?" challenged the teacher, "if the accents were equally strong?"

There was no response.

"How could you make two measures out of this pattern," she asked.

Now the solution of alternating measures of two and three beats was suggested, and put on the board by a student.

The selection "Three to Get Ready" by Dave Brubeck was presented at this point. It took several listenings to the first part of the composition to discover an introduction in three, followed by alternating sets of three-three-four-four. Students initially were asked to listen for the accents, or strong beats, and then to clap them softly. Next they were challenged to try to count silently between claps to determine whether the music moved in sets of three or four. Almost immediately someone said "three," but as the piece progressed, a look of confusion spread over many faces.

"It starts in three, but something happens," said Angela.

"Yes, something surely does happen," agreed the teacher. "This time raise your hand when you feel you can't count 'three' any longer."

Most of the class raised their hands within the first two measures of "four." Several caught the change immediately.

"This time," continued the teacher, "try counting 'four' when 'three' doesn't work."

With the next listening two perceptive children began to recognize the changing sets. The teacher then put the following metric progression on the board:

She pointed to the patterns as the class listened. The students seemed pleased to be able to recognize what was happening metrically.

The class liked the Brubeck music ("because it has a beat!"), and from this point on they were eager to create compositions that employed shifting meter and irregular meters. The greater challenge for the students, however, lay in playing the scores they had created.

Polyrhythm

The term *polyrhythm,* meaning "many rhythms," is used to refer to the simultaneous sounding of unlike rhythms. These may, as indicated earlier, involve different meters (technically, *polymeter*) or simply rhythm patterns with unlike accent. Such combinations create interesting and often very complex rhythmic sounds.

An easy introduction to polyrhythm is found in combining words with different numbers of syllables, and with natural accents which create unlike sets. For example:

As various groups of students clap such patterns simultaneously, accenting the first syllable of each pattern, they will hear the resultant, more complex pattern of accent. Soon they may be able to create and combine two meters without the help of words:

Clapping these rhythm scores or playing them on percussion instruments requires concentration, coordination, and the ability to maintain a steady tempo. The teacher may assist the students with respect to tempo by moving his hand in a beat of "one" to coincide with the metric beat.

Students also may experiment with the combining of various accent patterns within the same meter, as shown below. (Also see the example on page 115.)

None of the phrases in the examples on page 123 is complex in itself, but when combined with a second phrase, the resultant effect is interesting. After participating in experiences such as those suggested above, many students should be able to write simple polyrhythmic scores using both techniques described, and thus better understand contemporary compositions that utilize them.

Contemporary Percussion Composition

Many of the activities suggested in Chapter 2 as preparation for percussion composition can be adapted to irregular meter, shifting meter, and polyrhythm. Indeed, all endeavors in composing with percussion instruments may be considered contemporary, for during the last two decades percussion music has gained increasing recognition. Prior to 1945-1950 the percussion section of the orchestra had been considered primarily a "seasoning" for music—indispensible, but not capable of standing on its own. Within recent years, however, numerous works scored for percussion alone have been published, and available recordings of such works are growing in number. Compositions such as *Toccata for Percussion* by Carlos Chavez, *Concerto for Percussion and Small Orchestra* by Darius Milhaud, and *Ionization* by Edgar Varèse have become accepted as "respectable" music, providing additional justification, if needed, for encouraging percussion composition with students.

The strongest *educational* justification for such activity is the relative success with which children can "compose" with percussion instruments of indefinite pitch, or even with percussive sounds that they can create without instruments. Such composing in rhythm is not dependent upon a knowledge of basic harmony or a concern for melodic progression. Children can gain a sense of accomplishment through creating and playing extremely simple (or very complex) rhythm scores. These scores may be based upon irregular meters, combined meters, or no meter, as well as upon traditional ones.

The intermediate ungraded class was humming with excitement. The children had been exploring sounds of percussion instruments, including those of original instruments they had brought from home. They had, over a period of days, compared these as to their relative pitch, volume, resonance, and method of producing sound, and had grouped the assortment accordingly. The teacher had promised that today the children might begin to create their own percussion composition.

"In order to compose we must have a plan," explained the teacher. "We need a rhythmic idea. Can someone clap a rhythm pattern?"

A volunteer did so, clapping the following pattern:

The teacher asked him to repeat his pattern so that the class might imitate it.
"How could we write it down most easily?" questioned the teacher.
"With long and short lines," said Phillip, who then wrote on the board,

⸻ ⸻ ⸺ ⸺ ⸻ ⸻ ⸻

"Long, long, short, short, long, long, long," said the teacher as he drew the lines. "Let's count steadily as we clap, to see how many counts are in this set."

| One, | two, | three, | four, | five, | six |

⸻ ⸻ ⸻ ⸻ ⸻ ⸻

replied most of the group, although one or two started to count each clap.
"I think it would be more interesting if we made it seven," said Roxie, who had been fascinated by a percussion "Waltz" in $\frac{7}{4}$ time. (See page 120.)
"Yes, let's have seven," replied Roxie's friends. And so it was:

| 1 | 2 | 3 | 4 | 5 | 6 | 7 |

"Now how do you wish to use your instruments in this measure?" questioned the teacher.
After several suggestions were tried, the following groups of instruments were chosen:

| 1 | 2 | 3 | 4 | 5 | 6 | 7 |
| Ringers | | Rattles | | Drums | | Clappers |

Instrumentalists were chosen quickly to try out this first phrase. After brief practice, the pattern was played perfectly. Extreme difficulty arose, however, with the attempt to repeat the pattern without loss of a beat. It seemed natural to feel the set in "eight" instead of "seven" and the ringers had difficulty coming in without waiting for an extra count following the clappers.
"This is a fine beginning," said the teacher. "Before we leave the composition for today, let's write some music notes instead of these lines, so that we will have a more accurate record of this measure. How many different kinds of notes will we need?"
"Two."
"What kinds of notes shall we choose?"

The first suggestion was that half notes be used for the long sounds and quarter notes for the two shorter sounds.

As the teacher wrote the suggested notation,

she asked, "Then what will the meter signature be? There are seven counts to a measure. What kind of note are you giving one count?"

"It would have to be in $\frac{7}{2}$ time," replied a quick thinker, "but I've never seen any music in $\frac{7}{2}$!"

"It certainly is in $\frac{7}{2}$ as you've written it here," said the teacher, pleased that someone had recalled several discussions related to signatures of percussion accompaniments to songs. If someone wants to try to write it another way tonight, we'll take a look at it tomorrow."

But, no one remembered, and so the composition was continued on the next day—in $\frac{7}{2}$.

Examples of student compositions using irregular and shifting meters follow:

Grade One. The class clapped while a *soloist* played the second pattern on an instrument of his choice.

Long	Long	Long	Long	Long	
Short Short Long		Short Short Long		Long	

Grade Two. See Chapter 1, page 31.

Grade Three.

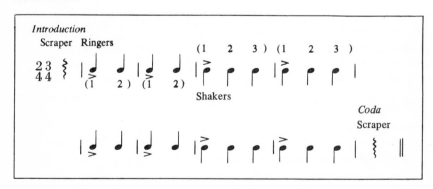

Grade Five.

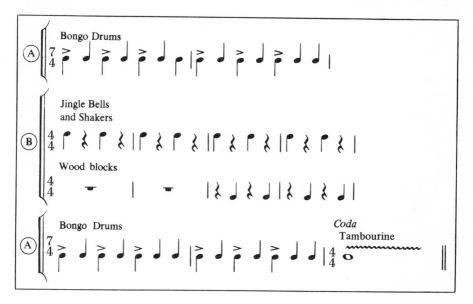

Grade Seven.

Newer Ways of Organizing Pitch

In an attempt to produce new musical sounds, contemporary composers have broken tradition in their use of pitch as well as rhythm. They have combined pitches in ways that completely defy eighteenth and nineteenth century rules of tonic-dominant harmony. One of the most fundamental points of departure has been the use of *pitch organizations* other than major and minor scales.

Some twentieth century composers have called upon old scale sources, such as the Church modes (see Chapter 3), to achieve a non-Romantic musical sound. Others have searched out exotic pitch organizations—those commonly used in certain non-Western music. Such scales include pentatonic (five-tone, often of equidistant intervals rather than half-steps and whole steps), whole-tone (six tones of whole step intervals), and microtonal scales (composed of intervals smaller than half-steps, and difficult for the Western ear to accept). Still other composers have attempted to find a new sound by creating their own scales from the half-steps within the octave. Some of these new scales have been "created" and used by a sufficient number of composers to have been classified as *synthetic* scales.

Children who have the opportunity to create their own scales will be more able to appreciate contemporary music built out of nonconventional scales and, as a related benefit, will strengthen their understanding of the construction of the more familiar diatonic scales.

Creating with Original Scales

Original scales may be created by nearly any age group, provided the term *scale* is loosely defined. In one second grade class, most of the children had learned to play "Mary Had a Little Lamb" on the black keys of the resonator bells, and some in the key of C as well. The teacher suggested that the children make scales of their own on which to play the tune. The class discussed the number of tones used in the song and observed that the first three were close together whereas the highest one was farther away. Various members of the class were then allowed to choose four tones on which to play the song. The results delighted the children, as the rhythm and words of the song were so familiar. The new sound of the song with each new selection of tones was irresistible. Several of the most interesting attempts were saved and the class enjoyed trying to sing them. An example is given on page 129, opposite.

A more exacting experiment was attempted with a seventh grade music class that had discovered they could develop scales that differed from the familiar major and minor. They had listened to short excerpts from *Windsong* by Harry Partch (using his 43-tone scale), *Two Studies on Ancient Greek Scales* by Partch, *Tabuh Tabuhan* by Colin McPhee (based upon five-tone scales), and *Four Strict Songs for Eight Baritones and Orchestra* by Lou Harrison (employing various pentatonic scales with retuned instruments). Then the class had considered the meaning of the term *scale*, and by process of elimination had deduced that a scale is "a sequential organization of pitches within the octave."

The students' exploration of original scales began with an assignment to

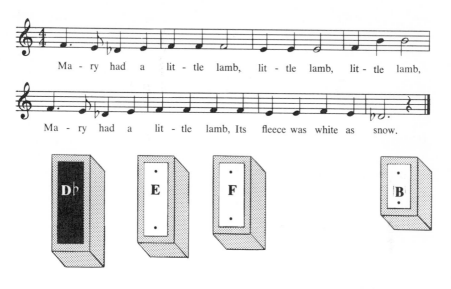

Ma - ry had a lit - tle lamb, lit - tle lamb, lit - tle lamb,

Ma - ry had a lit - tle lamb, Its fleece was white as snow.

It is fun to move the bells around to create original scales. It also is good for the ear.

create a seven-tone scale, starting on middle C and using each letter name only once. They were to avoid C major. The teacher had put an example of an original scale on the board:

C   D♯   E   F♯   G♯   A   B   C

Students who had access to pianos were encouraged to use them, and tuned bells were available for experimentation.

Nearly all members of the class completed the assignment. To the amazement of everyone, there were few duplications. The students had not imagined that so many possibilities existed. A few of the scales they developed were as follows:

C	D#	E	F#	G#	A#	B	(C)
C	D	E♭	F#	G	Ab	B♭	(C)
C	D♭	E	F	G♭	A	B♭	(C)
C	D	E♭	F	G♭	A♭	B♭	(C)
C	D♭	E♭	F♭	G♭	A♭	B	(C)
C#	D#	E	F#	G#	A#	B	(C#)
C#	D#	E	F	G	A	B	(C#)

The real interest developed with the next assignment, which was to transpose a familiar folk tune into these original scales. "Three Blind Mice" was suggested for a beginning, as it uses all seven tones of a scale. A duplicated copy of the song written in C major was given to each student, who was then to alter the version according to his scale. Students who were sufficiently motivated and capable were encouraged to go beyond this assignment and transpose other familiar songs originally written in the key of C. The transposed versions were played on bells, piano, or any instrument of the student's choice. Those who did not wish to play their tunes were allowed to ask another student or the teacher for assistance. Some of the songs proved to be quite interesting in their new framework; others were less so. Thus it was concluded that a composer might need to try out a number of possibilities before choosing the original scale that best suited his musical purpose.

Examples of "Three Blind Mice" set with original scales are given on the opposite page. Example No. 2, when analyzed, was discovered to be the dorian mode, transposed to C#. (See Chapter 3, pages 88-89.)

One of the most extreme examples in the creation of original scales is to be found in the work of Harry Partch. Mr. Partch has developed a scale consisting of 43 pitches to the octave, in contrast to the familiar 12 half-steps to be found in chromatic scales. The use of this microtonal scale obviously

necessitates not only a unique system of notation, but new instruments as well. For the past forty years Harry Partch has been creating, building, and assembling assorted instruments, and giving them unusual names. The sound of Mr. Partch's music, together with the story of his original scale and pictures of his instruments, is a source of fascination for both children and adults. Students are eager to search out objects with interesting timbres and then create music for them, after hearing and seeing the results of this composer's efforts. (See pages 110-112, 139, and "For Your Exploration" for titles and sources of Harry Partch's music.)

Exploring the Tone Row

During the first quarter of this century an Austrian composer named Arnold Schoenberg created an entirely new system for composing music. Although Schoenberg's intention was to extend the post-Romantic chromaticism of

Wagner, Brahms, and Mahler, his music soon showed completely new dimensions. In his effort to camouflage traditional tonality, he evolved a method for avoiding tonality (key tendency) altogether. He devised a scheme for creating a distinct *tone row* (series of tones) to serve as the raw material for each composition. Each row was to contain all twelve chromatic tones within the octave, with each tone being equal in importance. The order of the tones within the row was to govern the development and structure of the composition.

Originally Schoenberg decreed that to avoid any tonal implications no tone in the row could be repeated until all twelve had been sounded. This principle is not strictly adhered to in *serial* (based upon an original *series* of tones) writing today, although prolonged repetition is avoided, as is any placement of tones which would create functional triadic implication.

Although there does not appear to be a great deal of serial music that can be used at the elementary level for analytical purposes, there are some serially conceived compositions which are interesting to children and which can be used with success. Furthermore, it is not expected that elementary or junior high age students will understand more than the simplest underlying principles of serial music. On the other hand, it is not possible to consider a music curriculum balanced if the entire realm of twelve-tone technique is ignored. The impact of Arnold Schoenberg and of serial composition upon music of the twentieth century has been too great for this, and many composers who are not serial composers in the strict sense of the term have been influenced by the ideas behind the system. Most of the post-1950 work of the noted contemporary composer, Igor Stravinsky, has been serially conceived. Thus it would seem important to provide some exploratory experiences that would enable children at all levels to become acquainted with the sound of serial music and the idea of the *tone row*.

Tuned chromatic resonator bells were indeed a marvelous invention, for without them how could the sixth grade have experimented with the twelve-tone row so successfully!

The class had worked previously with pentatonic scales and therefore were acquainted with five-tone as well as seven-tone scales. They had discussed the characteristics of the tonal penta-scale (no half-steps) and had described its effect as "floating". There had been such high interest manifested in both tonal and semitonal penta-scales (see Chapter 3, pages 76-87), that the teacher felt the students would be enthusiastic about exploring another type of pitch organization. The teacher was not disappointed.

"How many different kinds of scales can you describe?" asked the teacher.

The students first mentioned the various pentatonic scales with which they had been working, and then added major and minor seven-tone scales. One student who had studied piano also recalled the term *chromatic* scale.

"All the scales you've mentioned have something in common," continued the teacher. "The seven-tone major and minor scales, especially, contain one tone which is more important than all others. What would it be?"

Many responded, "The home tone," "Number one," and "Do."

The teacher explained that a man named Arnold Schoenberg about fifty years ago wanted to create a completely new kind of pitch organization—one in which no tone would be more important than any other. He called his pitch organization a *tone row* instead of a *scale,* so that no home tone would be expected. The teacher suggested that the class experiment with the building of a twelve-tone row.

Twelve resonator bells—the chromatic tones from middle C# to the C above, inclusive—were removed from the box and scrambled. Twelve students were asked to take any bell, together with a mallet, and stand in a row without looking at the pitches of the bells. The row of tones was then played from left to right, and the result was greeted with approving laughter from those listening.

"We now have a melodic theme," explained the teacher, although melodies need not use all twelve tones of the row. Many melodies built from major or minor scales do not use all seven tones of the scale. Now, listen again to this tone-row tune to see whether anything is lacking."

"It doesn't have any beat" said Phyllis.

Sam said all the notes were the same length.

"It doesn't even sound like a melody to me," scoffed Julia.

The teacher continued, "What two things must every melody have?" reminding the class of previous discussions.

"Pitch and rhythm, and this row doesn't have any rhythm," exclaimed Tom with exuberance at this discovery.

"Right," encouraged the teacher. "This is really what Phyllis and Sam and Julia were saying too. We could add rhythm in a number of different ways. For a start, let's have each person put his pitch on the chalkboard staff, using either a quarter, a half, or a whole note. Start with the first person in the row. Will those with the black key bells please write the flat name instead of the sharp, just to be consistent.

This was the result:

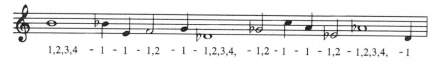

1,2,3,4 - 1 - 1 - 1,2 - 1 - 1,2,3,4, - 1,2 - 1 - 1 - 1,2 - 1,2,3,4, - 1

It happened that this row had an interesting contour and contained little triadic implication. Such is not always the case. The row was played by the twelve students with the quarter note used as the basic unit. Thus a quarter note received one count, a half note two counts, and a whole note four.

Having the count written under each note seemed to help the players. The bells were then given to twelve other students who played them in the same fashion.

On succeeding days the class learned more about the twelve-tone row. The most important rule, originally established by Schoenberg, was that no tone should be re-used until the entire row had been sounded, in order to avoid making one tone more important to the ear than any other. The teacher explained that there were four major forms of any row—the original (O), the retrograde (R), the inversion (I), and the retrograde-inversion (RI). When asked to deduce the meanings of these terms, one boy said, "Retrograde must mean going backwards, because that's what the retro-rocket does." The word *invert* was defined by another as meaning to "turn up-side-down." It then became obvious that retrograde-inversion would be a backwards and upside-down form of the row.

To further illustrate the meaning of inversion, the teacher drew the following diagram and used these few notes from "Hickory Dickory Dock" as an example of the inversion of intervals:

"like looking in a mirror
or a reflection in the water"

At another time the teacher played on the piano the retrograde and the inversion of "Here We Go Round the Mulberry Bush" and asked the students to discover which was which. The class was quick to hear that in the inverted form the pitches changed while the rhythm remained the same, and thus they decided that this form was more easily recognized. The retrograde changed both the sequence of pitches and the rhythmic structure of the melody. The three forms (O, R, I) of the melody are as follows:

The class was anxious to experiment more with the tone row. The teacher explained that figuring out the inversion was a rather tedious process for those inexperienced in working with intervals, but that anyone who wished to do this as an outside project would be welcome to do so. The retrograde was quite easy to prepare, however, as it involved playing the row already noted on the board by starting at the end and going backward. By borrowing a second set of resonator bells, it was possible to involve twenty-four children in playing the row and its retrograde:

At this point some listening material was introduced. A very easily identifiable row occurs three times in the "Bransle Double" section of a ballet entitled *Agon* by Stravinsky. A chart of the row used in this selection was shown, and the row was played on the piano.

TONE ROW FROM *AGON* [6]

The wide leaps were observed. Students were then asked to raise their hands each time they heard this row, as the short piece from the recording was played several times. The instrumentation is quite sparce, enabling the listener to isolate the row rather easily after the first hearing.

"Did you notice anything different about Mr. Stravinsky's row and yours?" inquired the teacher, "other than the order of the tones?"

"He broke the first rule—he repeated the first note and some others," remarked Sancho disapprovingly. At this point the teacher explained that Mr. Schoenberg had not objected to the immediate repetition of a note, but to the re-use of a tone out of the order of the row.

"That was a good observation, Sancho," she commended. "What else was different?"

"Well, his notes jumped around a lot more than ours," said Jane with a somewhat puzzled look. "How did he use just twelve tones?"

"There are some techniques of developing tone-row music that we haven't discussed as yet," explained the teacher. "Another of Mr. Schoenberg's rules was that any tone of the row could be used in any octave. Or, the tones could be displaced from their original octave. Thus the term *octave displacement* is used to describe this procedure."

"We could displace some of the notes in our tone row," suggested Steve.

"Yes, and we may need to do something else," the teacher added. "For example, if we displace the second note to the same tone two octaves higher, what problem will we have?"

After some thought the class realized that the resonator bells didn't go that high. "We couldn't play it," said Steve with disappointment.

"If we had a piccolo we could," encouraged Jill, who played the flute.

"We could play it on a piano, and even higher notes," responded Lily, who had just started to take lessons on this instrument.

"Do we have any instruments in the classroom which could be substituted for some of the resonator bells?" challenged the teacher.

With this question the class was launched into a consideration of *fragmentation*. It was pointed out that fragmentation could be achieved

[6] From *Agon,* by Igor Stravinsky. Copyright 1957 by Boosey and Hawkes, Inc. Reprinted by permission.

without octave displacement, that is, that interesting melodies could be constructed by giving tones to instruments with contrasting timbres even though the octave remained the same. The class then began to think of possibilities for fragmenting their tone row.

This school was one which did not have an abundance of music equipment. The resonator bells being used for the tone row were one of two sets in the entire school. The teacher had collected a number of percussion instruments of her own, and the children had become so interested in sounds that they had brought in some objects with unique timbres. The substitution of tones in a tone row, however, required instruments of definite pitch, so imaginations had to be stretched.

After considerable inventory, discussion, and offers of equipment from home, the following resources appeared to be available:

(A. H.)—Autoharp—strings to be plucked.
(W. Bl.)—Wood block—with a pitch approximating middle E.
(Mel. B.)—Melody bells—one octave set, xylophone type.
(Bell)—Small brass handbells, 2—approximating B and C above middle C.
(S. Fl.)—Plastic song flute.
(Uke)—Ukulele.
(G.)—Guitar (with one string broken).
(Pno.)—Toy piano.

When the last three items arrived at school, the possibilities of all instruments listed were explored, ranges were considered, and the class' tone row was then fragmented to the delight of all. The replacements were indicated on the score with the abbreviations shown in the list above; all other tones were played by resonator bells:

The preceding account has shown only a few devices which students can use to experiment with the development of a tone row. The rhythmic structure of a row may be arrived at in a variety of ways. A meter such as $\frac{6}{8}$ or $\frac{5}{4}$ may be chosen arbitrarily, and the row divided into three, four, or five measures. Or the twelve students may work in four groups of three each, to choose a meter and develop a rhythmic pattern for their measure. The result probably will be a theme with shifting meter. Other possibilities for extension of the row include playing it on a second set of bells in imitation (as a round). This requires strict adherence to tempo and is a challenge that older students enjoy. Another idea for exploration is to use the first six tones of the row and the retrograde of these as a melody, with the second half used in like manner as an accompaniment. Also, percussion instruments of indefinite pitch may be added for accompaniment.

Even a primary class can explore the tone row. One first grade class chose twelve bells as described in the preceding example, and then played their row several times to the rhythm of "Oh Where, Oh Where Has My Little Dog Gone?"

Regardless of the extent to which exploration of the tone row is carried on, it is important to remember that the art of serial composition is a highly complex one, and that children's activities constitute a bare introduction to this system of pitch organization. This realization makes it no less important that such exploratory experiences be provided in order for students to receive a balanced musical diet.

Discovering Octave Displacement and Fragmentation Through Familiar Music

This is a familiar tune. If it does not look familiar, it is because many of the tones have been displaced from their original octave into other octaves. As mentioned earlier, this contemporary technique is appropriately called *octave displacement*. The original tune may be recognized more easily:

The first version of "Mary Had a Little Lamb" was created by a group of summer school children ranging in age from eight to twelve. Their arrangement, however, not only put tones into different octaves, but also distributed the notes among various instruments—a technique called *fragmentation,* also described in the preceding pages.

The use of octave displacement and fragmentation are directly related to serial composition, but are by no means limited to it. One of the considerations of serial technique is, as stated previously, that any of the tones of a series may be used in any octave. When octave displacement is thus employed in instrumental composition, it is inevitable that certain tones of a melody will require instruments different from those playing other tones. Very high pitches will be given to instruments that can play in high registers, whereas very low tones must be played by other instruments. Octave displacement and fragmentation are responsible for the leaping, angular character of much music in the contemporary idiom. Students may be helped to gain some feeling for this quality of contemporary composition through experimenting with these two related devices.

The teacher of the summer school class began, "This composition is based upon a song that all of you know. However, I'll bet no one in the room will recognize it. If you *do* know what it is, raise your hand, but don't tell anybody your idea."

The first portion of "Afro-Chinese Minuet" by Harry Partch was then played, with no title given. Not one child even tried to guess the identity of the song. All looked puzzled.

With a second playing of the same brief portion, one girl and one boy raised their hands. The girl lifted hers a bit hesitantly, but the boy waved exuberantly.

"Paul must be our best detective," said the teacher, "but before we ask him to tell us what he heard, we'll listen to a little more of this piece. I think all of you will recognize the melody this time."

The theme "Happy Birthday to You" is presented in an obvious way the second time it is used in "Afro-Chinese Minuet." When the students heard it, they immediately burst with the title, and Paul confirmed that he had known it all along. When he was asked *how* he had been able to recognize it, he decided it was because of the familiar rhythm. The first portion of the selection was played once again, and many now said they could hear the well-known tune.

"What did Mr. Partch do to this old tune which made it hard to recognize?" asked the teacher.

There were a few guesses, but no one was certain.

Another musical example was presented. It was Stravinsky's "Greeting Prelude," an arrangement of "Happy Birthday" written for Pierre Monteux on his eightieth birthday. In this piece Stravinsky employed octave displacement and fragmentation, as well as imitation and diminution. However, because standard instruments were used, the tune was more easily recognized. The children identified the piece quickly, and then discussed the way in which the tones "jumped all over the place." The terms *octave displacement* and *fragmentation* were introduced in much the same fashion as they were to the sixth grade class working with the tone row. Following the explanation some of the children said they liked Harry Partch's arrangement better than Stravinsky's; others preferred "Greeting Prelude." Nearly all the class thought both versions more interesting than the "plain old tune."

Then the class eagerly went to work transforming "Mary Had a Little Lamb" through use of these two devices. This group had a much greater assortment of instruments available than did the class which used octave displacement and fragmentation to alter their tone row. The abbreviations used in the version given below represent the following instruments: [7]

(T. Bl.)—Oriental temple block.
(A. M.)—Alto metallophone.
(S. Gl.)—Soprano glockenspiel.
(Pno.)—Piano.
(Xy.)—Wooden xylophone.
(Ps.)—Psaltery.
(A. H.)—Autoharp, plucked strings.
(Bell)—Small metal bell approximating this pitch.
(Tutti)—All instruments having a G in any octave.

All tones not labeled were played on resonator bells.

It would be difficult to overstate the degree of enthusiasm that children of all ages, but especially upper elementary and junior high, exhibit when they are involved in the kinds of exploration described in the last two classroom

[7] For additional information regarding these instruments, see the Appendix.

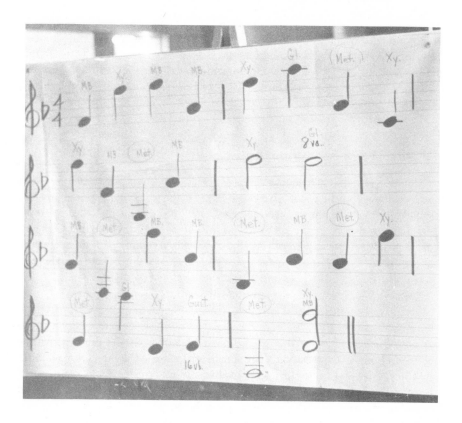

*Large charts may make children's compo-
sitions more meaningful to them.*

examples. It is important that all students have opportunity to participate in one way or another. It is also amazing to see the degree of patience that they will exhibit while waiting to be one of the 10 or 12 or 20 who will be next to play the tone row composition or the fragmented version of a familiar tune. There is a fascination in listening to the variety of timbres created by assorted instruments, and always an eagerness to play them. The execution of one of these original arrangements provides a challenge as well, for it is not easy to coordinate the rhythm of even a familiar tune, when each student is playing only one tone. For example, the most difficult responsibility in the fragmented version of "Mary Had a Little Lamb" (page 140) fell upon the person playing the third note, for it had to be sounded soon after the short second note. Thus, each child had to learn to think the rhythm of the familiar song and not just play his instrument after someone else played.

Beyond the values of developing rhythmic coordination and participating in a musical group endeavor, the ultimate goal of the activities described is to help students begin to understand some of the ways in which contemporary music is developed from thematic ideas. It may be wise to begin with familiar tunes and move into tone row experimentation. It also is important to relate listening examples that utilize the same techniques children are exploring, if significant musical growth is to occur.

Newer Ways of Combining Pitches

During the first millennium of the Christian era, music consisted of a single melodic line, usually *chant;* this music is referred to as *monophony* (a single sound). Gradually there evolved the practice of singing diverse tones simultaneously. This came to be known as *polyphony* (many sounds). The art of combining melodic patterns became increasingly complex, reaching a zenith in the *counterpoint* (note against note) of the sixteenth century. Focus still was primarily upon the horizontal, or melodic, aspect of music.

Toward the middle of the seventeenth century, composers became more concerned with the vertical aspect of music—the harmonic structure underlying the combination of melodic lines. This new emphasis upon tonal organization (key center) led to the rise of harmony as the prime structural consideration in composition. This practice dominated eighteenth and nineteenth century music writing. As tonality, or the concept of a key center, became firmly established, so did the desire to create musical interest through departure from expected harmonic progression. Harmonies grew more and more complex, through modulation and alteration of chords, until the entire tonic-dominant system was weakened. In revolt against this overmodulation, excessive chromaticism, and lack of resolution, twentieth century composers have deliberately opposed *traditional* harmonic practice and attempted to discover fresh sounds.

The bulk of music that has comprised the school curriculum during the first half of the twentieth century has been drawn from the Romantic era, despite the fact that composers since the turn of the present century have been moving in new directions. Many have returned to a linear concept of writing; this music is predominately contrapuntal rather than harmonic in texture. Harmony that does occur often defies the rules of the tonic-dominant system. Chords frequently are based upon intervals other than thirds. Groups of adjacent tones, called *clusters* may replace triads. Two or more keys are used simultaneously. It is important that children hear and experiment with both traditional and newer kinds of harmonic treatment. The former have been discussed briefly in Chapter 3. It is the purpose of this section to suggest a few ways by which children can explore new harmonic sounds.

The fifth grade had been studying the Colonial period in American history, and had learned several of the songs of the early settlers. One of these was "Old Hundred," more commonly known today as the "Doxology" ("Praise God from Whom all blessings flow"). As the teacher placed a recording on the phonograph, he said, "There is a familiar tune used in this composition. I am sure you will recognize the melody, but it may have a different sound for several reasons. See whether you can discover why the tune has a new sound."

The last section of "Trauermusic" ("Funeral Music"—for viola and strings), composed by Paul Hindemith, was played. The class identified the tune quickly, but many indicated by their expressions that they did not approve of its treatment.

"What did Mr. Hindemith do to change the sound of 'Old Hundred'?" the teacher asked, as he wrote the composer's name on the board. "In what ways was this different from the recording of the song we sing?"

"He made it sound gloomy," scoffed Virginia.

"It's awfully slow," added Greg.

The teacher continued, "The music sounded gloomy to Virginia. Perhaps the slow tempo that Greg mentioned contributed to the dreary feeling. What else gave the music this quality?"

"Was it minor?" asked Opal, recalling recent experiments with major and minor chords on the Autoharp and resonator bells.

"Yes, there were minor chords, as well as major chords throughout the piece," replied the teacher, "and many of the chords had tones added which made them neither major nor minor. Listen again and raise your hand each time you think you hear a major chord."

The class quickly discovered that it was difficult to distinguish chords because of "all the extra notes" (added tones, suspensions, and passing tones), but all agreed that the piece ended on a major chord. Other observations included (1) the viola (children thought it was a violin) playing solo interludes between phrases and often introducing minor sounds against a sustained major chord in the orchestra; (2) the change from duple to triple meter; and (3) the omission of several tones from the second phrase of the traditional melody. With repeated listenings the class began to feel that Mr. Hindemith's arrangement of "Old Hundred" was not so distasteful after all.

One day the teacher suggested that the class create some new harmonies of its own. "Sue," he said, "would you come and play 'Hot Cross Buns' in the key of C on the resonator bells?"

The class earlier in the semester had experimented with the playing of this three-note tune, starting on many different bells. They had done this by ear to reinforce understanding of the system of movable "do" and of the difference between intervals of a half-step and a whole step. Therefore everyone in the class could play this melody in at least one or two keys.

"Now, Jewel, please come and play the same tune with Sue, but use the black keys of the melody bells. You'll need only the group of three black keys," offered the teacher as a reminder.

As this class was accustomed to experimentation, they did not respond as negatively as some students do to hearing a song played in two different keys simultaneously. Most of the children were not particularly fond of the sound, however.

"This time, instead of the melody bells, try playing the same tones on the wooden xylophone," suggested the teacher.

The class showed amazement at the difference in the sound that resulted.

"That really sounds pretty good," exclaimed Norm in surprise. His peers agreed.

"What conclusion could you draw from this simple experiment?" inquired the teacher.

After some discussion the group decided that the total effect of a piece of music depends a great deal upon the instruments used. This concept was pursued further at a future time.

"Let's get back to our experiments with harmony," continued the teacher. "What did Sue and Jewel just do?"

"Played on two instruments at the same time," offered Pat.

"Is there anything new about that?" asked the teacher.

"We played the same song in two different keys at once," replied Sue, without waiting to answer the question.

"Yes," replied the teacher, "and this is one kind of harmony used by composers today. They often use two or more keys at the same time, and because of their interesting combinations of instruments, the music sounds less strange than we might expect."

As a conclusion to this simple experiment, the words *bitonality* (two keys) and *polytonality* (many keys) were put on the board and analyzed. On succeeding days the class used "Hot Cross Buns" and "Mary Had a Little Lamb" similarly in the following kinds of experiments:

- Combining many different keys and deciding that some combinations seemed more appealing, and some less appealing than others.
- Playing tunes at different intervallic distances, for example, a minor second, major third, perfect fifth, and drawing similar conclusions. (This is actually the same experiment as the one above, except that the emphasis is upon interval rather than key.)
- Playing a melody in one key over a repeated triad in another key.
- Combining a melody in its original form with the same melody in retrograde.
- Combining a melody in its original form with the same melody augmented in another key:

• Building chords based upon perfect fourths (2½ steps) and perfect fifths (3½ steps) rather than triads (1½ steps—minor third; 2 steps—major third), and playing a melody over these repeated chords:

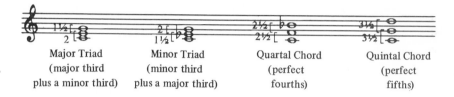

Major Triad	Minor Triad	Quartal Chord	Quintal Chord
(major third	(minor third	(perfect	(perfect
plus a minor third)	plus a major third)	fourths)	fifths)

• Building stacked chords (fixed-interval chords):

3rds   4ths   5ths

• Playing tone clusters (groups of adjacent tones) as accompaniment to tunes.

Although most elementary and junior high school classes will not have the time or musical background to pursue the study of contemporary harmony extensively, it is important that students of all ages have opportunities to hear a variety of kinds of harmonic treatment. If such experiences are not provided when children are young and in the process of forming aural concepts, the sounds of contemporary harmonies may meet stiff resistance at upper elementary and junior high levels. Such was the case with the junior high class that was presented with the challenge of setting a text modally (see Chapter 3, pages 92-94). Their desire was to change the characteristic modal tone to give the song either a major or a minor sound. Thus it would seem imperative to acclimate children to varied harmonic sounds at an early age.

The kindergarten had been singing the following song about a tiger:

THE TIGER [8]

WORDS AND MUSIC
BY GRACE BURLIN

The ti - ger walks a-round and 'round,_ His paws are soft,they make no sound _

But when he roars the build-ing shakes,_ So aw-ful is the noise he makes! _

Many of the children had dramatized the slow, stealthy movements of this large animal.

The teacher suggested, "We might have someone play music on the piano to accompany our tigers as they pace back and forth."

The class agreed eagerly.

"Would walking music for these tigers be on the low tones of the piano or the high tones?"

"Low, I guess, because he's so big and heavy," said Ronnie.

"Is the tiger in our song moving fast or slowly?" continued the teacher, in an effort to help the children verbalize the mood of the song.

"He can't go very fast, 'cause he's in a cage," sympathized Pablo. "That's why he roars!"

"Who would like to play some low, slow music on the piano? Armand, perhaps you could use the palms of your hands to walk on the piano keys, as our tigers walk around the room. Try to feel as though your hands are the tiger's paws."

With this guidance Armand was able to play some wonderfully effective tone clusters to accompany the song and dramatization. As others in the class had an opportunity to play the accompaniment, the change in dynamic level within the song was stressed, and the tone clusters became louder when the tiger roared.

Although these kindergarten children did not understand that they were using *tone cluster* harmony, and although the clusters were improvised in random fashion, the class was exposed to the sound of a kind of accompaniment which differs markedly from an accompaniment consisting of I, IV, and V_7 chords. This type of experience should help children be a bit more ready to listen perceptively to tone cluster harmony in the music of composers such as Charles Ives and Henry Cowell.

[8] From *Music for Early Childhood,* by Osbourne McConathy, et al. Copyright 1952, Silver Burdett Company. Used by permission.

There are many ways of playing "tiger music" on the piano.

Newer Directions in Musical Exploration

Today's composer is continually searching for new means of musical expression. In his attempt to create new sound sources, he is altering existing instruments, and creating new ones. The latter pursuit has caused him to turn to other fields, primarily electronics, for completely new musical media. Since World War II, tape recorder music, electronic music, and computer music have begun to evolve.

Although most of the work in the field of electronic music requires sophisticated equipment not available to elementary and junior high schools, there are recorded examples of electronically produced music which may fascinate children of all ages. In addition, it is possible for students to experiment in a limited way with tape recorder music.

A nonoriented observer might have questioned the purpose and value of the activities being carried on in this junior high music class. He would have witnessed one boy unwinding a short roll of magnetic tape and cutting it into pieces one or two feet in length. Two girls and another boy were picking up the pieces at random, and then carefully assembling them into a long strip with splicing tape. This scene was being repeated by two other groups. On the opposite side of the room a cluster of students were recording on tape a sequence of vocal and instrumental sounds which included the singing of one verse of "I've Been Working on the Railroad."

When the first group finished its splicing, the teacher asked the class to stop work for the day and return to their desks. This was done with great reluctance.

"Group One has finished splicing their tape, and would like to give it a trial run," explained the teacher. "Let's listen to it before they tell us how they produced it."

As the reconstituted tape was played, the class broke into sporadic peals of laughter from the pleasure of hearing such unexpected sounds. The teacher laughed as well, especially after one long, unanticipated period of silence. The group looked puzzled, but finally came to the conclusion that one piece of tape had been attached wrong-side-out. This potential pitfall was noted by the other groups.

"Now, Denny, please tell us what your group did to achieve this sound collage," requested the teacher.

"Well, we started with a bunch of sounds—it was really part of that percussion piece we wrote. We changed some of the instruments, and added some sounds with our voices. Then, after we recorded it on the tape, we cut up the tape, and spliced the pieces together, with some end pieces first. We recorded it at 7½ speed, and played it back at the slow speed. And that was it!"

"Do you think you'll make any changes in the piece?" questioned the teacher.

"Well, I don't know," replied Denny. "We'll have to talk about it. We could change that blank spot, but it's a lot of trouble to take it apart, and anyway, it sounds pretty interesting the way it is."

Prior to the tape recorder project, the teacher had introduced the subject of electronic music. In response to the request of several students to study some "modern" music, the teacher (without giving titles) had played portions of *A*

Poem in Cycles and Bells for Tape Recorder and Orchestra by Luening and Ussachevsky; *Gargoyles* (for violin and synthesizer) by Luening; "Ragtime" from *Evolutions* by Badings; and the first movement of *Contrasts* by Raaijmakers. "This is some *very modern music*," the teacher had commented as she presented the selections.

Although this was not the modern music the students had had in mind when they made the request, they found themselves intrigued by the variety of sound which had been produced by electronic means. It was explained that sounds in nature and man-made sounds could be recorded, and then altered by various means, such as changing speed, reversing direction, and taping over previous sounds; or that electronically produced sounds could be recorded and altered in a variety of ways.

Some of the students who were especially interested in science did some individual research and made reports to the class. After the tape-composition experiments had been completed by the class, several of the students commented that they thought producing a composition such as *A Poem in Cycles and Bells* must require a great deal of knowledge, time, and effort. The task of the serious composer was now more fully appreciated by all who had taken part in the "tape collage" project.

Even a primary class can experiment with alteration of recorded sounds. A simple percussion composition or a song sung by the class can be taped and the tape then played backward. Or the sounds on a familiar recording may be altered by playing the disc at a different speed (but using the needle originally required by the recording). Even the simplest involvement in the alteration of sounds by electronic means may help develop in young people an awareness of the kinds of experimentation being undertaken by many of today's composers.

The range of experimentation in the creation of new musical sounds and forms is too broad for discussion here or in elementary and junior high classrooms. It is vitally important, however, that both teacher and students be aware that such exploration is taking place. The most extensive experimental work is in the field of electronic and computer music. The use of microtonal scales, discussed earlier in relation to the work of Harry Partch and others, undoubtedly will achieve new emphasis and perspective through the potential of computers. Percussion composition, referred to extensively in Chapters 2 and 4, will be extended in timbre and form by electronic means. Other experimental efforts include the *chance* or *aleatoric* music of John Cage and others, and attempts by men such as Gunther Schuller and Lukas Foss, working from different points of emphasis, to incorporate into concert music the improvisatory freedom which characterized early jazz.

There are those who feel that the results of all such experimentation should not be dignified by the term *music*. Others insist that it is electronic music that most truly reflects the computerized age in which we live. Only time will reveal the lasting value of what is now experimentation. Meanwhile, teachers must recognize their responsibility to guide their students into the exploration and discovery of many kinds of music, so that they may eventually be capable of distinguishing the musical wheat from the chaff.

CONCEPTS RELATED TO CHAPTER 4

1. The human being tends to accept the familiar and reject the unfamiliar.
2. The term *contemporary music* refers to twentieth century music that utilizes the media and the components of music in *nontraditional* ways.
3. Many of the devices employed in contemporary music are borrowed from music of the past and music of non-Western cultures.
   a. Contemporary music makes extensive use of syncopation, irregular meter, shifting meter, lack of meter, and polyrhythm and polymeter.
   b. Contemporary music is based upon systems of pitch organization (scales) which differ from major and minor. These include the church modes and exotic scales such as pentatonic and microtonal.
4. Some contemporary music is developed from original scales, or original systems of pitch organization, primarily the tone row.
5. Contemporary composers often use devices of melodic alteration not known in traditional music, such as octave displacement and fragmentation.
6. Much contemporary harmony is based upon intervals traditionally thought of as dissonant.
7. New media for musical creation and expression are being found in the field of electronics.
8. The lasting value of music from any period can be judged only through time.

FOR YOUR EXPLORATION

With New Timbres—Encourage students to:

• Listen to music which utilizes new and unique sounds; relate these to familiar instruments.
• Use familiar instruments in new ways.
• Create original instruments.
• Develop compositions for these instruments.

With Newer Rhythms—Encourage students to:

• Sing songs and listen to music based upon irregular, shifting, and syncopated rhythms.
• Experiment with various means of creating syncopation.
• Create rhythms that utilize irregular and shifting meters.
• Analyze the subgroupings (subsets) in irregular meters.
• Combine rhythms with unlike accents to produce polyrhythms; combine rhythms in different meters to produce polymeter.
• Create and orchestrate rhythm scores that incorporate newer rhythmic devices.

With Newer Pitch Organizations—Encourage students to:

• Create original scales; transpose familiar tunes into these scales.
• Develop twelve-tone rows and utilize them in various ways.
• Explore inversion and retrograde.
• Experiment with octave displacement and fragmentation; transform familiar tunes by using these devices

With Newer Harmonies—Encourage students to:

• Listen to familiar tunes harmonized in new ways.
• Accompany songs with random tone clusters.
• Play songs in two or more keys simultaneously.
• Build chords using intervals of fourths and fifths instead of thirds.

With Newer Directions in Music—Encourage students to:

• Experiment with the alteration and manipulation of recorded sounds.
• Experiment with various kinds of chance music.
• Keep ears and minds open.

With Recordings* mentioned in this chapter:

Badings, Henk, "Ragtime" from *Evolutions* (Epic BC 1118).
Brubeck, Dave, *Three to Get Ready* (on *Time Out*, Columbia CS 8192).
Brubeck, Dave, *Unsquare Dance* (on *Time Further Out*, Columbia CS 8490).
Cage, John, *Amores No. 1* (on *Concert Percussion*, Time 8000).

*Because of the rapidity of change in availability of commercial recordings it is suggested that a catalog or a record dealer be consulted before ordering recordings listed here.

Chavez, Carlos, *Tocatta for Percussion and Orchestra* (Columbia CMS 6447; HBR 21003, 2 records).

Copland, Aaron, "Circus Music" from *The Red Pony (Children's Suite)* (on *Adventures in Music*, Gd. 3, Vol. 1, RCA Victor).

Cowell, Henry, *Banshee* (on *Sounds of New Music*, Folkways FX 6160; and Composers Recordings Inc. CRI 109).

Harrison, Lou, *Canticle No. 1* (on *Concert Percussion*, Time 8000).

Harrison, Lou, *Four Strict Songs for Eight Baritones and Orchestra* (The Louisville Orchestra LOU 58-2, 840 Fourth Street, Louisville 3, Ky.).

Hindemith, Paul, *Trauermusic (Funeral Music)* (Angel S-36484).

Luening, Otto, *Gargoyles* (on *Columbia-Princeton Electronic Music Center*, Columbia MS 6566).

Luening, Otto, and Vladimir Ussachevsky, *A Poem in Cycles and Bells* (Composers Recordings Inc., CRI 112).

Milhaud, Darius, *Concerto for Percussion and Small Orchestra* (Capitol HBR 21003, 2 records).

Partch, Harry, *Afro-Chinese Minuet* (on *Plectra and Percussion Dances*, Gate 5 Records, Issue C; recording and illustrated booklet available from Source Magazine, 330 University Ave., Davis, Calif.).

Partch, Harry, *The Wayward* (Gate 5 Records, Issue B, see first Partch entry).

Partch, Harry, *Two Studies on Ancient Greek Scales* and *Windsong* (on *Thirty Years of Lyrical and Dramatic Music*, Gate 5 Records, Issue A, see first Partch entry).

Raaijmakers, Dick, *Contrasts* (Epic BC 1118).

Russell, William, *Waltz* (on *Concert Percussion*, Time 8000).

Stravinsky, Igor, "Bransle Double" from *Agon* (Victor LSC 2879; Columbia CMS 6022).

Stravinsky, Igor, "Greeting Prelude" (on *Stravinsky Conducts Favorite Short Pieces*, Columbia CMS 6640).

Stravinsky, Igor, *Rite of Spring (Le Sacre du Printemps)* (Columbia MS 6319).

Varèse, Edgar, *Ionization* (Columbia MS 6146).

Part B

A Summer Experiment with the Academically Talented

"The music doesn't just grow bigger and bigger. It's kind of young and it grows older and older."

"Our composition has too much variety—it needs to hang together."

"May I take that record home? I have to study it to find my cue for the lightning."

So said a fifth, a fourth, and a third grader—members of a summer school experimental class in music.

The Setting

The experimental program described here was developed to study the extent to which elementary children could understand musical structure, through (1) their own composing, and (2) creative dance, or movement, to music.

The beginning composition experiences were limited to work with percussion instruments of indefinite pitch and to work with tonal penta-scales, both of which avoid harmonic problems inherent in diatonic composition. The dance experiences utilized music that exemplified simple musical forms appropriate for children's composition. An academically talented group was chosen for the program, as it was recognized that such children could absorb a great many ideas with comparative rapidity.

It was decided that a classroom teacher should be invited to participate in the program with the music specialist, in order that some of the results might be incorporated into the regular program during the ensuing year. In addition some guidelines for the class were established:

1. The class would consist of the following:
    (a) Twenty or fewer students, so as to give individual help and see as much growth as possible in a relatively short time.
    (b) Third, fourth, and fifth graders only. It was felt that this group should be old enough to write simple notation and move in the direction of beginning composition, yet young enough to participate in creative dancing without reluctance.
    (c) Academically talented and gifted students, as determined by individual I.Q. test scores of over 130, and teacher evaluation of academic achievement. Musical training and talent were not to be a consideration in making the selection of students.
2. Major emphases of the program would be as follows:
    (a) Rhythms, or creative dance, that first would free children to express their feelings and ideas naturally, and then would be used as a medium for interpreting form in musical composition.
    (b) Exploration of percussion as a means of developing sensitivity to and understanding of rhythm and timbre, and later as a medium for composition.
3. Time allotment would be two hours per day for six weeks.

4. Physical facilities would include two kindergarten rooms, a cafeteria for dance, and a small adjoining room. This amount of space would permit small group and individual work, as well as large group sessions.

There were no preconceived specific goals and there was no established course of study. The major objectives were to offer an enriched music experience for capable learners and to see how far these children at this age level, under rather ideal conditions, could progress musically. The six-week session more than justified initial expectations.

THESE WERE THE CHILDREN

Name*	Grade Just Completed	Chronological Age		I.Q. Test Score†
Harriet	3	9 yrs.	10 mo.	134
Tommy	3	9	2	140
Freddy	3	9	1	144
Elaine	4	10	3	130
Betty	4	10	0	157
Diane	4	10	2	147
Morris	4	10	3	133
Nanette	4	10	6	148
Steve	4	10	2	150
Alicia	4	10	8	131
Richard	5	10	8	147
Trina	5	10	6	130
Esther	5	10	7	132
Kirk	5	10	8	146

*Fictitious names are given.
†Stanford Binet Form LM or California Test of Mental Maturity.

Discovering the World of Sound

The first two weeks were devoted largely to exploratory activities. They began with a discussion of sound. The first challenge to the children was to think of all the different kinds of sounds they had heard. The children responded with the following: the song of birds, boat whistles, the zing of the jump rope, the sound of babies crying, the squeak of shoes, the rustle of paper, the sound of a drum and of a flute. They listened for a moment, sitting absolutely still, to see whether they could be completely *soundless.* They were aware, however, of the clock, the gardener outside, and the distant droning of a plane. The class then discussed the need for sound, and the ways in which human beings unconsciously tune in or out the sounds around them. The teacher pointed out that the ability of babies to imitate sounds is the beginning of musical learning. This brought quite a response from the group, as they recalled a little brother's or sister's continuous shrieking, pounding, and imitating of anything and everything heard. Someone said, "But that's noise," which started a discussion of pleasing and unpleasing sounds—and of music vs. noise.

After listening to several informative recordings about sound, the class decided that a distinguishing factor was whether or not an individual *liked* the sound, and that under varying conditions the same sound could be both noise and music to the ears. Later the section on music and noise on the recording *The Science of Sound* by Bell Telephone Laboratories further developed this concept.

Harriet asked, "What makes sound?" Several children thought they knew the answer.

Richard said, "Sound is vibration. Our eardrums pick up the sound and send it to the brain by way of the auditory nerve."

Stimulated by earlier discussions, the children discovered that they could *feel* the vibrations from one drum through another. They experimented to find out how far away the vibration could be picked up on another drum. They discovered that in some cases vibrations were felt when the second drum was as far away as another room. The children were bubbling over with vibrations the first week!

They experimented with other instruments, and found that some resonated longer than others. Those instruments available to them were chromatic individual resonator bells, two-and-one-half octave melody bells, sleigh bells, triangles, sand blocks, maracas, cymbals, finger cymbals, claves, guiros, Oriental temple blocks and other wood blocks, Autoharps, the piano, and a variety of drums including double bongos and a conga.

At the opening of school many of these had been placed on a table beneath a bulletin board displaying related pictures, record jackets, and the caption, "Can you find membranophones and idiophones?" This center provided food for thought and conversation for several weeks. Finally, after much research, several of the children were able to define both of these classifications of percussion instruments. They found that membranophones are those with a striking surface of membrane or skin, primarily the drum family, while idiophones have a striking surface of metal or wood. The children spent much time in experimenting with ways of obtaining sound from the instruments and in distinguishing between their various tonal qualities. These discoveries were to be of value later in their compositions.

During the second week of the program an oscilloscope was brought into the room and the children then saw sound waves. Discussion, research by the children, and aid from the *Science of Sound* recording developed a new vocabulary and new understanding. Words such as *sound waves, molecules, compression, rarefaction, frequency,* and *cycle* were used daily. The children wondered why some sounds appeared higher or lower to the ear than others. The science recording also answered some of these questions concerning pitch. Thus the group was gaining a new awareness of and sensitivity to the world of sound.

Finding Freedom to Move

The present culture places a premium upon conformity. Consequently it does not provide an atmosphere in which creativity, especially in movement, flourishes easily. Thus it seemed apparent that the children would need to acquire the freedom to listen and respond naturally to ideas and feelings inside themselves before any truly creative dancing could be seen. It was felt also that the acquisition of such freedom in movement would foster creativity in the total program.

A specialist in creative movement was invited to work with the group one hour a day for seven days. She took the children into the large room that had been used as a cafeteria during the regular session. There was plenty of space in which to move. Teacher and students sat on the floor, and next to them were a phongraph, recordings, and several baskets of surprises.

The teacher said, "Today we are going to have some fun with music. We are going to dance. This kind of dancing is already inside of us; all we have to do is turn it on under our ribs."

Some bouncy music was played. The teacher, capitalizing upon the children's excitement with their discovery that sound was vibration, spoke about letting vibrations from the music flow through their bodies. Several children said they already could feel it. At the teacher's invitation the children began to clap to the music. Soon most of the students got to their feet and showed some movement. The teacher then brought the children together and talked about an imaginary ball inside them which could bounce. Listening to the strongly rhythmic music again, they tried to feel the bounce inside them and attempted to let it take them up off their feet.

Next they talked about tying a string to the top of their heads and pretending they were puppets. They tried to dangle and bounce as puppets do. The teacher said, "Your feet can have balls in them too. Let them hang loosely and bounce easily." Now was the time for one of the surprise packages to be opened. The children were delighted to see an array of little Indian bells strung on elastic. The teacher gave the children bells to put on their feet; these helped them become less self-conscious. The music was a Navajo Indian dance. The children had found their feet.

During succeeding sessions other surprise packages were opened. One contained beautifully painted fans. The children were delighted. The teacher said to them, "Fill yourselves so full of music that it will spill from each fan." She played Japanese koto music. As the group talked about their dancing, they spoke of the wonderful things they had discovered their hands could do.

While the group listened to some Israeli songs, the teacher asked what kinds of motions they felt in this music. Harriet said, "It feels like twisting and turning." The contents of another surprise box made the twists and turns more much fun. This box was filled with scarves—scarves of many different sizes and colors.

With the playing of a "Sicilian Tarantella," the children were encouraged to let the bounce come out of their legs and arms so that they could bounce and twist right up into the sky. From this music came wonderful turns and leaps. Some of the children now were responding with a great deal of freedom.

The children were continually encouraged to "dance in their own way." The teacher talked about the music already within them, and about a "third ear" that listened way down inside them. In the beginning the children had been very reluctant to move. They had been self-conscious and afraid of ridicule. Their first movements were stiff, stylized and imitative of television or movie dancing. Soon, however, they were able to tune out the things around them—other children, their physical surroundings, even the fear of what friends would think—and tune in to the music inside themselves. It was at this point that *creative dancing began.*

On one occasion when the return of some superficial movements with hands and arms was noted, children were asked again to clap to the music, not with hands and arms alone, but from deep within. They found that the bounce inside could come out into their hands, and that they could clap in many places and in many ways. They could even clap without making sound. It was easy to see which children were feeling the rhythm with their entire bodies.

The children then were asked to line up against the wall and wait for the music to *pull* them out into space. Suddenly they were dancing alone and without self-consciousness. Now they were free enough for a more structured interpretation of music through movement.

Exploring Rhythm and Meter

A caption on a bulletin board read, "Where do you find rhythm?" Around this were arranged pictures of buildings, snow scenes, starfish, sedimentary rocks, and fabrics. The children had many responses to offer.

"There's rhythm in trees when the wind blows," said Trina.

"What about water patterns at the beach, after the waves break and the ripples crawl up the sand?" echoed Elaine.

"Well, there certainly is rhythm in music," offered Richard, who was an accomplished violinist. "What about the hands of a conductor?"

"To sum it up," said Freddy, "it's *motion*."

Other rhythmic impressions recalled were sea gulls' wings in flight, the sway of tall grass in the breeze, the beautiful curve of a man-made bridge. The children were aware that these rhythmic impressions could be *seen, felt,* and *heard.*

The teacher then spoke of measured motion, or the sense of recurrence as in the waves at the beach. She read from A. A. Milne's "Buckingham Palace." Nanette picked up the rhythm on a drum after the poem had been read. Soon all were able to sense where to come in for the refrain, "says Alice." The teacher then read some Japanese poems called Haiku. Several of the children were fascinated with these writings, which challenge the imagination by suggesting only the outlines of a picture. A comparison of the two selections revealed that, while rhythm could be felt in both, there was a marked difference. "Buckingham Palace" was built on a steady meter with regularly recurring accent. The Japanese writings, on the other hand, seemed to flow with an abstract, irregular, unmeasured rhythm. This discovery was then transferred from literature to music, as the group contrasted the rhythm of "Sicilian Tarantella" with that of "Clair de Lune."

The exploration of regular rhythm was pursued by clapping. The teacher clapped a pattern such as

and the children repeated it without losing a beat. Patterns in the same meter were relayed back and forth between teacher and students, and children were asked to count to themselves as they clapped. The teacher varied the note pattern each time, keeping within the established meter; for example:

This game was played using groupings of two, three and four. Children soon were able to identify the grouping by listening for accents and trying to count. They also were able to initiate patterns and move from one to another without losing a beat. It became quite a challenge to see how many different patterns could be clapped within a meter before a repetition was detected.

The next challenge was to try to write these rhythmic patterns in musical notation. This was very difficult for the children at first. Even those who could *tell* the meaning of a meter signature and perhaps read a rhythm pattern already written were uncertain in translating their own rhythms into writing. Through a discussion of how meter could be discovered by finding the natural accent (although the kind of note representing the unit, such as a quarter note or eighth note, could not be determined), most of the children became fairly adept at creating and recording simple patterns. The interest was so great that it was difficult to move beyond this activity. The youngsters were delighted, however, at the suggestion of "drumtalk" and quickly transferred their rhythms from clapping to drums and other instruments.

It had been observed from work with previous groups that instruments were handled more successfully when rhythm had been felt first through clapping and other movement, and this was shown now in the comparative ease with which these children used the instruments. As they began to play their individual rhythm phrases together, they were able to hear interesting resultant effects, especially when instruments with different timbres were used. After one such effort Freddy commented, "That sounded kind of like a new piece we played in orchestra last spring—without the melody, of course."

Diane then volunteered, "If we wrote those rhythms down, we'd have our own orchestra piece." The group was on the threshold of composing!

Finding Form in Composition

Although singing was not emphasized in this program because of the limitation of time, a few minutes each day were spent in this activity. Several enjoyable rounds led quite naturally into a discussion of contrapuntal music. Thus the idea of using the familiar canon as an approach to form in composition seemed wise at this point.

The children by now were intrigued with their writing of phrases in rhythm. Four of these using the same meter were put on the chalkboard:

These phrases were clapped and played consecutively as a single composition. Then instruments were chosen to represent four different timbres—drums, triangles and finger cymbals, tone blocks and claves, and guiros—and the composition was played as a four-part canon. The group was delighted with the results. Other such compositions were created and played by small *ensembles*—trios or quartets, depending upon the length of the canon.

Even at this stage some guidelines for composing were needed. The meaning of *phrase* was discussed, and the importance of rest or *cadence* mentioned. The two fundamental principles of composition—*unity* and *variety*—became part of the daily vocabulary. The group began to judge their efforts, and those of established composers, by these criteria.

Much learning about rhythm notation also was occuring. Many of the children had had no experience in writing notes and thus needed help in knowing where to put stems, how to write a meter signature, how to make rests. They learned the necessity for lining up measures when parts were to be played simultaneously. Orchestral scores were brought in to aid in this regard, and also to show at a later time what kinds of symbols might be used in scoring for certain percussion instruments.

Discovering Musical Form Through Movement

The first emphasis in developing freedom of movement with this summer school group had been upon the mood or character of the music used. The teachers had worked for an emotional response which would release the children to express their feelings. Now that this was taking place, the children were ready to approach the music intellectually, or analytically, to find out how it was put together. The teacher began to work for recognition and interpretation of themes.

No title was given for the next selection that the teacher had chosen to present. She simply said, "The composer of this music painted a beautiful picture in sound. Listen to see what time of day you think it might be." The opening strains of "Cloudburst" from Ferde Grofe's *Grand Canyon Suite* brought varied response.

Some said, "Evening," as the music was so quiet; others responded with "Early morning." After hearing more of the selection, however, they decided it must be morning, for the music seemed to "awaken." Soon they heard the storm, and were amazed that they could hear thunder and lightning and wind and rain. "What a clever composer!" said Betty. Later when they recognized a return of some of the first themes, they knew the storm had passed, leaving in its place a bright new day.

The group worked with "Cloudburst" for a twenty- to thirty-minute period each day for three weeks; movement and listening activities were alternated frequently within each period. After many listenings to find themes, after identifying these themes with ideas such as dawn and thunder, and after trying out certain kinds of movement that seemed to fit the ideas best, a simple choreography evolved, built upon the following sequence:

A—Dawn (the very beginning of day).
B—Flowers awakening (a brighter feeling).
C—Sun's rays (spreading and warming the earth).
D—Clouds (beginning to cover the sun—a quiet, suspenseful theme).
C—Repeat (sun returns temporarily).
D—Repeat (clouds completely blot out the sun).
Storm section, including thunder, lightning, wind, and rain.
C—Return of the sun, brighter than ever.

THEMES FROM "CLOUDBURST" [1]

At the beginning of the work with "Cloudburst," the teacher encouraged all of the children to interpret each of the thematic themes. Gradually, as the individuals chose to be identified with certain themes, the movements became more organized and refined, although there was caution lest anyone revert to stereotyped patterns. *There were no steps developed.* The movement was free and spontaneous, even though through repetition it assumed form within the framework of the story sequence.

[1] From "Cloudburst," Fifth Movement from *Grand Canyon Suite* by Ferde Grofe. © Copyright 1931, 1932 Robbins Music Corporation, New York, N.Y. Copyright renewal 1959, 1960 Robbins Music Corporation, New York, N.Y. Used by permission.

One of the least well-coordinated children—a boy who had found it difficult to move freely—insisted on portraying the delicate "A" theme, and became completely absorbed as the dawn.

Diane and Nanette chose to dance the flower theme.

Kirk identified the four smooth phrases of the third theme, and suggested that four children might be used, one for each ray of the sun.

Harriet and Richard became great round clouds, which seemed to swell with moisture before the storm.

Betty and Alicia whirled in recurrent motion as the wind brought on the rain.

Tommy, who asked to take the record home to "find my cues for the lightning," made long, wonderful leaps. Elaine demonstrated lightning with marvelous angular arm motions.

Morrie said that thunder should have a bumpy, heavy feeling, and proceeded to demonstrate.

After one evaluation the dawn, flowers, and sun's rays remained on the floor during the storm, and writhed back and forth as if tossed by the elements. As the storm subsided they rose and danced with gladness, while the elements of the storm disappeared.

Freddy, a budding artist, offered, "Hey, if I could have a few volunteers to help me, I could build a frame out of wood and tack on a sheet, and paint some background scenery." Although the teacher was anxious not to rely on any physical props this enthusiasm could not be dampened, and thus several days later there appeared a 9' x 12' display of clouds and sun.

It *did* provide the finishing touch!

One of the most popular pieces of music to which the children danced was "Polka" from the *Age of Gold* ballet suite by Shostakovitch. The children loved its Raggedy Ann, loose-jointed feeling. The group charted the themes. The children were surprisingly accurate and quick to catch new themes or variations of ones already heard. When the children were asked what the music suggested to them, and *why*, there were many replies.

"It sounds like Martian people dancing, or stick people," said Trina. "There are no curves in the music."

One of the boys thought it sounded like busy traffic noises and began to identify various vehicles suggested by certain timbres. Other ideas were a dance of the instruments, a haunted house, a puppet shop, a carnival, and people dancing in a forest. Children always were asked to justify such ideas by referring to the content or construction of the music itself.

Another child (whose real name was Peter) felt certain that this must be a scene from the court of Peter the Great. Following his suggestion that various themes could indicate the entrance and performance of various buffoons, the children chose their own places and gave a fine interpretation of the music.

The second movement of the *"Clock" Symphony* by Haydn was introduced to demonstrate the use of a repeated simple motif as a unifying element in a composition. The children quickly caught the repeated "tick-tock" as being the unifying pattern, and also heard the contrasting violin melody played above it. The children spoke of many kinds of clocks they had seen and of different ways of showing repeated motion.

Esther said, "The clock should be moving steadily in a circular pattern, while those interpreting the violin melody should be dancing around it." This selection was not pursued beyond showing the two contrasting kinds of motion. The repeated pattern, however, was to be used soon in the composition work.

Kodaly's "Prelude to a Fairy Tale" from his *Hary Janos Suite* was used to illustrate theme and variation. The children discovered that this music was not composed of several themes, but that the same melodic material was treated in a variety of ways. They decided that the single theme gave the composition unity.

When asked what created variety, Trina replied, "The theme kept growing higher and higher. It kept changing register."

Freddy added that the interest was kept alive by a change in dynamics.

Richard commented that the music seemed to him "like a pod opening. Most pods grow from side shoots, but this one grew right out of the top. When the brass played, the pod burst open."

Most of the children found a place on the floor and portrayed the growth of this music by unfolding, rising slowly, and stretching outward. Betty, however, sat for a moment and reflected, "You know, that music doesn't just grow bigger and bigger. It's kind of young and it grows older and older."

The children often became tired from strenuous movement. At such times the teacher had them lie on the floor with plenty of room around them and played quiet music such as Debussy's nocturnes, "Clouds" and "Sirens." The children would close their eyes and pretend they were as light as clouds floating through the sky. Sometimes they would pretend they could breathe under water and that the water was slowly flowing over them, sometimes turning them over. This kind of activity relaxed the children and helped develop their powers of concentration.

Although the children had interpreted much music that was light and airy, it was difficult to make a transition from a light feeling to a heavy one. The teacher played "Pantomime" from Kabalevsky's *Comedians* and asked children to think of the heaviest thing they knew. Answers were troops in the army after a battle, a dinosaur, a blue whale, a penitentiary, Jupiter, a steel building, and a large animal. One child was disturbed by the reaction she had to the music. She said it gave her an eerie feeling, the kind of feeling she got from watching science fiction television programs. The children took their places on the floor, trying to concentrate on the weight of the particular thing they had envisioned. As a result, many were able to show heaviness in their movements.

The last musical selection to which the group danced was "Spring" from *The Seasons* by Vivaldi. The children charted the themes, and quickly found the piece to be in rondo form, as it kept returning to the original theme. This form had been discussed only a few days before in connection with their composition work. At that time the group had listened to several short rondos. The form of "Spring" was recorded by the children as follows:

$$A - B - A - C - D - A \text{ (in minor)} - E - A - F - A$$

One child caught the place where the original theme was repeated in minor instead of major. Although the main theme (A) was recognized as it returned each time during the first listening, subsequent hearings were required before it could be determined whether any of the contrasting sections was repeated. It was finally decided that there were five contrasting sections. Harriet was interested in the section in which two violins were playing, with one imitating the other. She felt that two children should be dancing at this point.

The children decided among themselves which ones should represent the various themes. A relatively large number were used for the main theme—A—to which the music returned repeatedly, and other themes were danced by individuals or by two or three students together. All arranged themselves around the periphery of the room and were able with little direction to come in at the correct time. It was interesting to realize that although this music contained a story element not unlike "Cloudburst" (that is, a spring day interrupted by a storm which soon passed), the children now were much less concerned with the story than with the actual thematic changes in the composition. There was little discussion of the programmatic aspect of this selection. Interest now centered in the *structure of the music itself.*

As the teacher observed this beautiful interpretation of form and mood in fine music, she could not help but marvel at the growth that had taken place. Those who six weeks before could barely clap or move were now listening intently for a new theme that would carry them into the flow of creative expression. She knew that not only had these children found a new freedom within themselves, but that the music they had encountered through movement would be theirs for life.

Discovering the World of Composition

At the beginning of the fourth week of school pentatonic scales were introduced to the children through the black keys of the piano. After experimenting with this scale the children called it "magic," for no one could play a "wrong" note using only these keys. In fact two or three or four people could improvise at the same time with pleasing results; there were no dissonant or clashing sounds as there were when the same was attempted on the white keys.

Students found that a pentatonic scale like the black key scale could be built by starting on any note of the keyboard and making the pattern of intervals the same. After discovering that this scale corresponded to the first, second, third, fifth, and sixth degrees of a major scale, and after discussing half steps and whole steps, the children built many of these five-tone scales containing no half steps. They delighted in choosing a starting tone, finding the correct five pitches, and improvising freely on melody and resonator bells. For fun they tried creating some "space music" and were enormously pleased with the results.

At the beginning of the exploration of this new pitch organization, the teacher asked, "Do these black key melodies remind you of music from any particular part of the world?" Most of the children mentioned countries from the Middle or Far East, although one said, "Brooklyn." Elaine said it sounded a little like the music she had heard while watching Japanese dancers on television. The class then recalled and sang the Chinese pentatonic song, "Lotus Blossoms," and created an introduction and simple accompaniment for it on the bells. They found that five of their Oriental temple blocks approximated a pentatonic scale beginning on D.

The greatest excitement of the six weeks was generated with the presentation of some new German-made instruments (see the Appendix):

1. An alto xylophone, with a range from C below middle C up an octave and a sixth.
2. An alto metallophone, with the same range as the xylophone.
3. A soprano glockenspiel with a pure celestial quality; it's range was from C above middle C up an octave and a sixth.

These instruments contained removable wooden or metal bars within the diatonic ranges given, plus F#'s and B♭'s. From this time until the close of summer session the teacher was plagued by children inventing excuses to practice on the new equipment. Much care was exercised each day by those who brought out the instruments and later put them away.

The class now was anxious to compose a pentatonic piece. After serious consideration of which pentatonic scale to select, they chose D so that the temple blocks could be used to advantage. The notes of the scale were D, E, F#, A, and B. Four-four meter was selected, and with music paper and pencil

in hand once more, the children went in pairs to write four measures of pentatonic melody. Each pair had the use of some kind of bells.

The greatest problem in composing at this age level is that children's ideas usually surpass their patience and ability to record them. Thus the teacher was amazed at the completeness of several of the melodies that resulted from this effort. Rather than use these intact for the first section of the composition, however, she decided to take something from each child's work. This delighted the children. Section A (shown below and on page 170) opened with a gong part, followed by a melodic pattern for melody bells, and one for alto metallophone. The two melodic patterns were continued as ostinatos throughout the sixteen-measure melody which was played on the alto xylophone.

It was now necessary to decide how long the whole composition should be, and in what form. The children could see that section A consisted of an introduction, melody "a," melody "a" repeated, melody "b," with a return to "a" (aaba). In planning a second section, the group discussed the need for

OUR PENTATONIC COMPOSITION

unity and variety. One student suggested keeping the same key because the temple blocks hadn't been used as yet. This seemed logical to the others.

After due consideration it was decided that variety could be created by having more instruments play at the same time, thus producing a different texture, and by changing the meter to $\frac{6}{8}$. Six instruments were chosen, melody and countermelody assigned to two, and accompaniment patterns to the remaining four. The class again worked in groups of two to write eight measures for section B of the composition (shown opposite). When the resultant parts were played simultaneously, the effect was very satisfying.

The teacher was grateful at this point for the ABA form, because she wanted to move on to another endeavor, and yet felt it important to finish this effort. Kirk saved the day by asking, "Why couldn't we go back to part A? It sounds real good!"

Esther added that they could play the melody on a different instrument the second time, and Diane thought the introduction could be put at the end for a coda. "The gong really should be at the end as well as the beginning," she added.

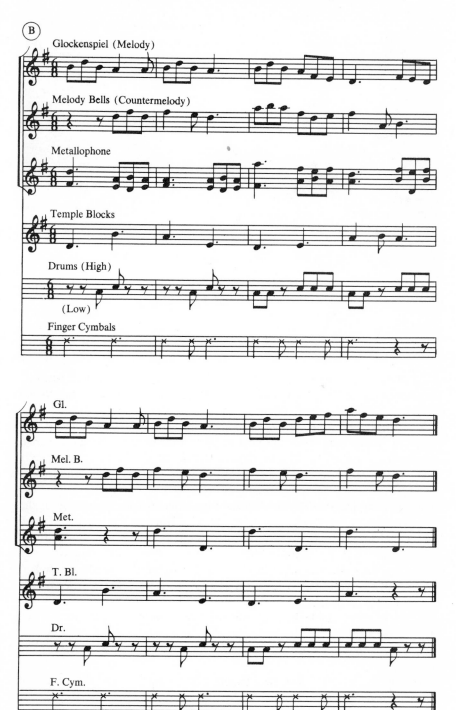

As for a title, suggestions were "Five-tone Melody," "Pentatonic Sonata," "Composition in D Pentatonic," and "Moonlit Sonata." The class finally settled for "Our Pentatonic Composition."

The terms *song form, canon, introduction, interlude and coda, theme and variation, sonata,* and *rondo* by now had taken on meaning for the children. Rondo form seemed to offer an opportunity for small groups to write short sections that could be used in a composition with little alteration. The teacher decided to return to the medium of percussion of indefinite pitch. The children were interested in using rondo form after charting the themes of the Vivaldi rondo for dancing. (See pages 166-67.) Three-four meter was selected and a goal of eight measures set for each group. The class divided into groups of two and three by choosing those with whom they could work well, and then they were asked to select instruments that would be interesting together. The representative choices were a surprise, as there were several of each kind of instrument available.

Kirk and Morrie took the guiro and two wood blocks, one high-pitched and one low-pitched.

Harriet, Alicia, and Esther decided upon double bongos, maracas, and triangle.

The claves, maracas, and two temple blocks finally were the choice of Nanette, Elaine, and Trina.

Freddy, after having much difficulty in working with his original group, withdrew to a secluded spot with sand blocks and wrist bells. Later he complained, "My part just *has* to have some bongos to make it finished," and so it had!

Tommy, Betty, and Diane seated themselves on the floor with a tambourine, bass drum, double bongos, finger cymbals, and large cymbals. Tommy, keeper of all cymbals for his group, devised a new sound by propping one large cymbal upside down between two pieces of wood and hitting the cymbal with a mallet.

Richard, a dedicated composer who worked laboriously at home on bell and piano pieces, had a strong conviction that some melody should be provided (on the large metallophone, of course). He felt that it would "break the monotony and really add both unity and variety." Thus he developed the following melody, which, it was later decided, should be played on the wooden xylophone sometimes and occasionally omitted:

Three of the groups wrote their sections with little or no help. Two groups needed a great deal of assistance in recording the desired notation. From an examination of the completed score, which follows on pages 175-79, it will be apparent that just two of the sections were finished with eight measures only, whereas the others were sixteen, sixteen, and fourteen measures in length.

Each of the groups rehearsed its music and then performed it for the rest of the class. There were not many suggestions for improvement, for the children seemed quietly impressed with the success of their efforts and were most appreciative of the contributions of their peers.

The decision as to which should be chosen for the main rondo theme (to be repeated after each other section) was difficult. Finally the part with the greatest variety of instrumental sounds (group 5), including the xylophone melody, was entitled "A." Two sections were combined as "C" because each seemed short when played alone. Placement for all was determined by instrumental quality or color.

The finale came after the first playing of the entire composition. True to the tradition of composers, and typical of a very creative little boy, Tommy said with excitement,

"Hey, I have a *great* idea for a coda. Listen to this!"

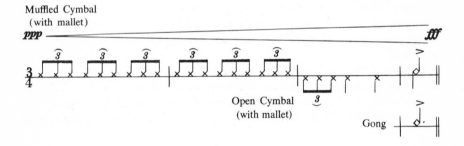

—and with it, "Rondo Fiesta" was completed.

RONDO FIESTA

for Percussion Instruments

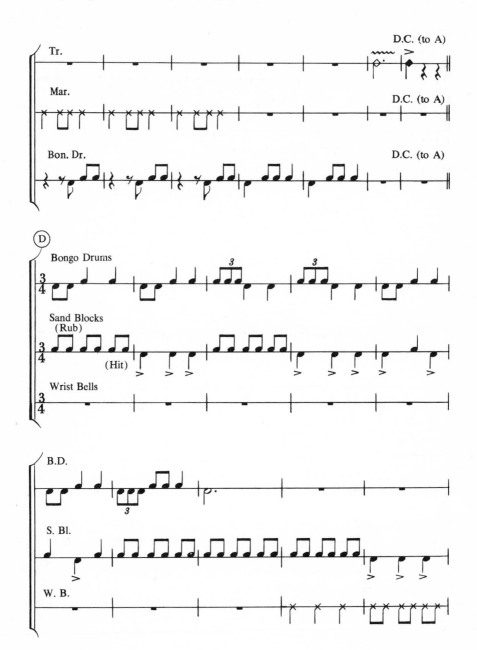

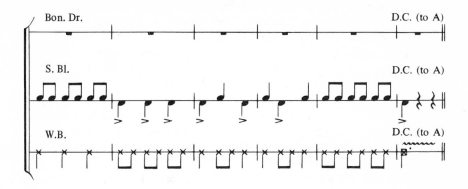

Coda

Cymbals (Suspended)

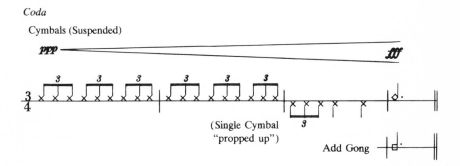

Implications

The experiment just described was carried on with a selected group of gifted students. Similar activities also have proved highly successful with classes of average and below-average ability. The major difference between groups is the speed with which new ideas are grasped, thus affecting the rate at which work can progress. It also appears that the melodies and rhythms created by gifted children show more variety and originality than those of students of lower ability. This may result from a broader experiential background in music on the part of those who are classified as *gifted*.

The potential for developing musical understanding through combined percussion composition and creative movement experiences seems unlimited. The approach is both educationally and musically sound for children, for the following reasons:

1. It offers opportunities for learning through first hand participation in, experimentation with, and creation of music.

2. It utilizes a wide range of individual interests and abilities in group endeavors, making it ideal for multigraded or ungraded situations, as well as for the single-grade class.
3. It provides a meaningful framework for unlimited academic learnings in areas such as (a) musical form or structure; (b) rhythm in music; (c) the notation of music; and (d) simple principles of composition.

Acquisition of such learning will put children well on their way to music literacy. Moreover, the understandings and skills acquired in this manner are not likely to be superficial, for students will have found them essential tools for their own creative endeavors.

Today's children are this nation's future explorers in music as well as in science. How well prepared will they be?

Appendixes

Classroom Instruments

The creative activities described in this book have utilized a variety of instruments, the majority of which belong to the percussion family. Although some percussion instruments, such as resonator bells, produce tones of definite pitch, the larger number make sounds of indefinite pitch. Instruments of this type have been available in many schools for years, and descriptions and illustrations of them are given in most of the current music textbook series, as well as in commercial catalogs. Thus some instruments are mentioned here by name only.

Percussion Instruments of Indefinite Pitch

The numbers in the illustration below correspond to the numbers in the following list:

1. Drums (assorted sizes and types)
2. Sand blocks (3/4" x 3 1/2" x 8")
3. Castanets on a handle
4. Sleigh bells
5. Triangle
6. Wood blocks (assorted sizes and types)
7. Tambourine
8. Jingle clog
9. Finger cymbals
10. Cymbals
11. Cocoanut shells
12. Gong

The following Latin American instruments, though available in many schools, may be less familiar to some teachers than the previous group. The numbers in the photograph correspond to the numbers in the list below:

1. **Maracas** (*mah-rah'-kahs*)—A pair of shakers made of small gourds or wood, and filled with seeds or small pebbles. (Plastic maracas are not recommended.) Usually played by alternating hands and using a wrist motion; young children may find it easier to tap a single shaker against the palm of the hand.
2. **Guiro** (*(g)wee'-roh*)—A long gourd, cowhorn, or wooden cylinder with notches or grooves cut around the middle or along one side; played by scraping the grooved area with a thin wooden or metal stick.
3. **Cabaca** (*cah-bah'-sah*)—A round gourd with wooden handle attached, or a double-bulb gourd, surrounded by a network of beads and/or seeds; played by resting the instrument in one hand and, with the other hand, twisting the gourd inside the beads. Produces a swishing sound.
4. **Double bongo drums**—A pair of small drums of contrasting size and pitch, fastened together; usually played while held between the knees so that both hands may be used for striking the drum heads. (When purchasing, check to see that the larger drum has the lower pitch.)

5. **Claves** (*cla'-vehs*)–A pair of hardwood sticks, usually about 1″ in diameter by 6″ in length; played by resting one stick across the fingers and thumb of a closed hand and striking the other stick against it. The clave tone block, which simulates the timbre of this instrument, is easy for young children to play.

6. **Cowbell** (without a clapper)–Frequently used in Calypso music; available in various sizes with various pitches; played by striking with a mallet.

7. **Castanets**–A pair of small, concave wooden clappers; those attached to handles are most easily played, by pointing the instrument toward the floor and shaking, or by striking the head of the instrument against the palm of the hand (see Number 3 in the illustration on page 184). A **handcasta** (shown here) is also easy to play.

8. **Conga drum** (not shown)–A large conical shaped drum, usually suspended by a shoulder strap; should produce a deep, resonant tone.

Tuned Classroom Instruments

The following instruments, which have been mentioned in the book, are shown in the illustrations on these two pages.

1. **Resonator bells** (*front*)—Individual bells consisting of metal bars fastened to hollow resonator blocks; played by striking with rubber tipped mallets. Available in chromatic sets, usually from middle C to the G an octave-and-a-half above, although an additional five bells below middle C are available and desirable.

2. **Autoharp** (*center*)—A stringed, chording instrument, played by pressing bars that dampen certain strings, and then strumming so that the remaining strings will resonate. A similar instrument is the Chromaharp, including the Caroler model which possesses a wider range of chords than the Autoharp.

3. **Melody bells** (*rear*)—Also called **songbells**; metal bars fastened to a single frame; usually 1 1/2 or 2 octaves in range; played by striking with a rubber-tipped mallet.

4. **Oriental temple blocks** (*below*)—Originally carved for use in Chinese temple worship. May be bought in sets of five, tuned to a pentatonic scale, or may be purchased as individual blocks. (The pitches should be checked before purchase, as the commercially made blocks often do not approximate a familiar pentatonic scale.)

Courtesy of Peripole, Inc.

The following instruments are German-made by two major companies,[1] which call their products Studio 49 and Sonor. The instruments are available in diatonic sets with added F#'s and B♭'s, and also in chromatic sets. Instruments described below (and referred to throughout the text) were chosen because they produce *timbres* that offer contrast to the more familiar classroom bells and also provide contrast in *register.* The bars are removable, making it easy for young children to play isolated tones or groups of tones and facilitating the experimental building of scales by students of all ages.

1. **Soprano glockenspiel**—Produces a clear, ringing sound that will carry above resonator and melody bells. The photograph below shows diatonic (*left*) and chromatic (*right*) glockenspiels.

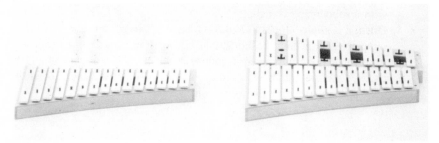

Courtesy of Peripole, Inc.

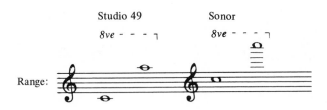

Range:

Studio 49

Sonor

---

[1] Some American Manufacturers also are experimenting with similar instruments.

2. **Alto metallophone**—Has a rich, resonant timbre which also provides a contrast to resonator and melody bells.

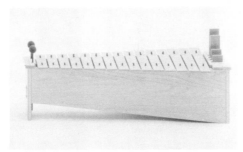

Courtesy of Peripole, Inc.

Studio 49   Sonor
(ALTO METALLOPHONE)   (TENOR-ALTO METALLOPHONE)

Range:

3. **Alto xylophone**—Provides a crisp, wooden timbre in contrast to the resonating sound of all metal instruments. Shown below are chromatic *(left)* and diatonic *(right)* xylophones. Soprano and bass xylophones are also available.

Courtesy of Peripole, Inc.

Studio 49   Sonor

Range:

Glossary

accent. Stress or emphasis given to certain tones; may be regular (normally recurring, that is, *pulse*) or irregular (imposed on normally unaccented tones; see *syncopation*).

affective domain. Attitudinal area of learning.

augmentation. Doubling the duration of a given rhythm (opposite of *diminution*); for example,

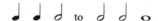

canon. A form of music similar to a round and based upon imitation.

chord. A specific formation created by combining three or more tones in a prescribed manner; for example, a triad.

chromatic scale. The progression of twelve equidistant half steps within the octave:

cluster. See *tone cluster*

coda. A section at the end of a composition, following the main body of the music.

cognitive domain. The intellectual area of learning.

concept. A meaning which remains with the learner following a given experience.

contrapuntal. A style of music that is linear, or melodic in its construction, rather than harmonic; from *counterpoint,* meaning *note against note* or melody against melody.

creativity. A thought, act, or product that is original to its producer.

descant. A countermelody (second melody), which may be sung or played simultaneously with a given melody; usually higher than the melody it accompanies.

diatonic. A seven-tone scale, consisting of five whole steps and two half steps, as found on the white keys of the piano; lacking chromatic tones.

diminution. Halving the duration of a given rhythm (opposite of *augmentation*); for example:

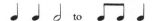

dynamics. The gradations of volume or degree of loudness in music.

form. The structure or organization of music; refers to both the external forms of music and the internal design within music.

fragmentation. The contemporary device of giving various tones or portions of a melody to different instruments.

Haiku. A form of Japanese poetry consisting of seventeen syllables and divided into three lines of five, seven, and five syllables respectively.

harmony. The simultaneous sounding of two or more tones.

homophonic. A musical texture that is predominately chordal; music in which a melody is supported by a vertical, or chordal, accompaniment. (Opposite of *polyphonic.*)

imitation. The restatement of a theme in different voices (parts), with overlapping created by voices starting at specified points in the given theme; the basis for round, canon, and fugue.

improvisation. Music performed extemporaneously.

interlude. Music inserted between stanzas of a song or sections of a larger work.

interval. The distance between two tones; named by counting both tones involved; for example:

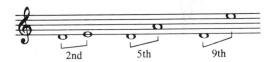

introduction. Music that precedes the main body of a composition.

irregular meter. Compound meters based upon odd-numbered combinations, such as $\frac{5}{4}$ and $\frac{7}{8}$, and falling into irregular groupings of two's and three's. (For example, $\frac{9}{8}$ might consist of regular groupings of 3 + 3 + 3, or irregular groupings of 2 + 2 + 3 + 2.)

major scale. A seven-tone scale consisting of half steps and whole steps, with half steps occurring between degrees 3 and 4, and 7 and 8; for example:

melody. A succession of pitches that move in time and express a musical idea.

meter. The organization of rhythm in music, established by natural accent and measured by bar lines; the measuring of undifferentiated beats into groups, or sets.

minor scale. A seven-tone scale characterized by the occurrence of a half step between degrees 2 and 3, and classified into various types, including the following:

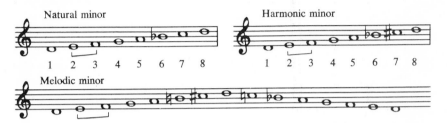

microtonal scales. Scales comprised of intervals smaller than half steps.

mode. Broadly defined, any kind of scale, such as major, pentatonic, hexatonic. More strictly, the ecclesiastical or medieval church modes—diatonic scales based upon the white keys and built by starting on any key and playing the seven tones within the octave.

modulation. Change of key within a composition.

octave displacement. The contemporary device of moving any tone in a melody from its original octave to a different octave.

ornamentation. The embellishment of a tone or group of tones by means of trills, turns, and the like.

ostinato. A repeated pattern; may be of definite or indefinite pitch.

pentatonic. A five-tone scale; most commonly, those containing no half steps (tonal penta-scale), and those containing one or two half steps (semitonal penta-scale).

percussion. The group of instruments played by striking, shaking, or scraping; some produce sounds of definite pitch, whereas many others are of indefinite pitch.

polyharmony. The simultaneous use of chords from two or more keys.

polyphonic. A musical texture that is predominately melodic, or linear, in construction; created by combining more or less independent melodic lines. (Opposite of *homophonic.*)

polytonal. Music that employs two (bitonal) or more keys or tonalities simultaneously.

psychomotor domain. The motor-skill area of learning.

pulse. Normally recurring stress or accent.

register. The range of voices or instruments; for example, *upper register.*

retrograde. The use of a theme in reverse order, beginning at the end and progressing backwards.

rhythm. The organization of duration, consisting of pulse, pattern, and meter.

rhythmic pattern. Any grouping of long and short sounds and silences.

rondo. A form of music, consisting of a recurring section, with two or more contrasting sections; for example, ABACA or ABACABA.

scale. An ascending (and descending) order of tones governed by a specific scheme of intervals; originally derived from melody, and subsequently forming the raw material for composition.

serial. Referring to music based upon one or more *tone rows,* or series of tones, and governed by compositional principles of *twelve-tone technique.*

set. A grouping; in rhythm, may refer to a measure—a grouping of beats into two's and three's, multiples of two or three, or combinations of two and three; when the set (measure) consists of more than three beats, it may be divided into subsets.

shifting meter. The changing of meter within a section of music.

sound effect. The reproduction or simulation of environmental sounds, both natural and man-made.

structure. Form or organization of music.

syncopation. The result of displacing accent, that is, accenting normally weak beats or portions thereof.

tempo. Rate of speed.

ternary. Three-part form, labeled as ABA.

texture. The distinguishing character of the music resulting from the ways in which the vertical and horizontal elements are combined.

timbre. The characteristic quality of the sound of a voice or instrument; its tone color.

tonality. The sense of key, created by a tonal center (tonic), or tone to which all others are related.

tone cluster. A chord comprised of three or more adjacent tones.

tone row. A designated order, or series of tones (usually 12), without a tonal center, that serve as the raw material for serial composition—a system of composition devised by Arnold Schoenberg.

transposition. Transfer of music from one key to another.

Bibliography

Austin, William W. *Music in the Twentieth Century.* New York: W. W. Norton & Company, Inc., 1966.

Bloom, Benjamin S. (ed.). *Taxonomy of Educational Objectives.* Handbook I: "Cognitive Domain"; Handbook II: "Affective Domain." New York: David McKay Co., Inc., 1966.

Bruner, Jerome S. *On Knowing.* Cambridge: Harvard University Press, 1962; New York: Atheneum Publishing Co., 1965.

Bruner, Jerome S. *The Process of Education.* Cambridge: Harvard University Press, 1965.

Copland, Aaron. *Music and Imagination.* Boston: Harvard University Press, 1952; New York: Mentor Press, 1959.

Crocker, Richard L. *A History of Musical Styles.* New York: McGraw-Hill Book Company, Inc., 1966.

Dallin, Leon. *Techniques of Twentieth Century Composition.* Dubuque: Wm. C. Brown Company, 1964.

Dorian, Frederick. *The Musical Workshop.* New York: Harper and Row, Publishers, Inc., 1947.

Driver, Ann. *Music and Movement.* New York: Oxford University Press, 1966.

Experiments in Musical Creativity. Washington, D. C.: Contemporary Music Project/Music Educators National Conference, 1966.

Gary, Charles L. (ed.). *The Study of Music in the Elementary School—A Conceptual Approach.* Washington, D. C.: Music Educators National Conference, 1967.

Haldeman, Eloise Ann. *Developing a Comprehensive Musicianship Program for Children from Kindergarten Through Grade Six.* (Unpublished Master's thesis. University of Southern California, School of Music, June 1968.)

Hanson, Peter S. *An Introduction to Twentieth Century Music.* Boston: Allyn and Bacon, Inc., 1961.

Henry, Nelson B. (ed.). *Basic Concepts in Music Education.* The Fifty-seventh Yearbook of the National Society for the Study of Education. Chicago: University of Chicago Press, 1958.

Kneller, George F. *The Art and Science of Creativity.* New York: Holt, Rinehart and Winston, Inc., 1965.

Lowenfeld, Viktor, and W. Lambert Brittain. *Creative and Mental Growth.* New York: The Macmillan Company, 1970.

Machlis, Joseph. *Introduction to Contemporary Music.* New York: W. W. Norton & Company, Inc., 1961.

Maynard, Olga. *Children and Dance and Music.* New York: Charles Scribner's Sons, 1968.

Nallin, Walter E. *The Musical Idea.* New York: The Macmillan Company, 1968.

Persichetti, Vincent. *Twentieth Century Harmony.* New York: W. W. Norton & Company, Inc., 1961.

Rufer, Josef. *Composition with Twelve Notes Related Only to One Another.* 3rd rev. ed. Trans. by H. Searle. New York: The Macmillan Company, 1965.

Salzman, Eric. *20th Century Music: An Introduction.* Englewood Cliffs, N. J.: Prentice-Hall, Inc., 1967.

Self, George. *New Sounds in Class.* London: Universal Edition, 1968.

Slonimsky, Nicolas. *Lexicon of Musical Invective.* New York: Coleman-Ross Co., 1965.

Torrance, E. Paul. *Education and the Creative Potential.* Minneapolis: University of Minnesota Press, 1963.

Torrance, E. Paul. *Guiding Creative Talent.* Englewood Cliffs, N. J.: Prentice-Hall, Inc., 1963.

Witty, Paul, James B. Conant, and Ruth Strang. *Creativity of Gifted and Talented Children.* New York: Teachers College, Columbia University, 1959.

Zirbes, Laura, *Spurs to Creative Teaching.* New York: G. P. Putnam's Sons, 1959.

Index

Accent, 44, 57, 64
definition, 66
in determining metric organization, 93, 122, 160-61
in irregular meter, 119-120
in polyrhythm, 113, 122-23, 151
in syncopation, 57, 66, 113-16
in words, 47
Accompaniment
chordal, 98, 100, 101, 103, 106
pentatonic, 77, 85, 87, 105, 168, 170
percussion, 18, 19, 22, 50-55, 59, 67, 87, 97, 121, 126, 138
tone cluster, 145, 146, 151
tone row, 138
Aleatoric music, 149
Art and music, 36, 40-44, 66
Augmentation, 64, 98, 144-45
Aural perception, development of, 12, 13, 17, 33, 34
in contemporary music, 108-109, 145

Beat, *see* Pulse
Blank notation, 24-25, 29, 50, 67, 125, 126

Cadence, 61, 63, 162
Canon, 85, 127, 161-62, 172
Choric speech, 14; *see also* Speech
Chromatic scale, 76, 130, 132
tones of, 88,
use in Romantic music, 131-32, 142
use in tone rows, 132-33
Clapping games, 53, 56-57, 67

Clave pattern, 116
Coda, 29, 51, 59, 61, 63, 64, 77, 85, 86, 170, 172, 174
Components of music, 5-6
Compositions of students, *see* Scores, student-created
Concepts, lists of, 33, 65, 104-105, 150
Conceptual learning, 4-5, 6, 39, 40, 49, 57, 94, 98, 144, 145
Contemporary music, 107-152; *see also* Newer sounds in music
Countermelody
based upon a common tone, 101-104, 106
definition, 101
pentatonic, 170
Creativity in music, 2-4

Descant, definition, 101; *see also* Countermelody
Descriptive music, 22-23; *see also* Programmatic music
Diatonic scales, 26, 69, 76, 128
creating with, 87-94, 106, 155
definition, 105
Diminution, 98, 140
Discovery, 1-5
Dramatic play, 69
Dramatization, 13, 19-20, 34, 146; *see also* Movement, rhythmic
Duration
a component of sound, 5-6, 12, 33
of instrumental tone, 34
in melody, 76
organization into rhythm, 48, 57, 66
Dynamics, 5-6, 49, 103, 112